IMAGES
of England

THE
EAST SHROPSHIRE
COALFIELDS

A group at one of the outcrop workings at Foxholes, Benthall, during the Coal Strike of 1912. The portly lady in the centre is obviously playing a leading role as she holds both a sack and a riddle. The boy sits on a sledge as used underground locally. Women, girls and young boys played an active part in Shropshire mining but normally only on the surface. At least five female workers have been killed in accidents at Shropshire mines since 1860, the last in 1880. (D. Oakley)

NAMHO

The National Association of Mining History Organisations was founded in 1979. It is a registered charity (No.297301) that promotes the interests of those seeking to preserve the relics and history of our mining past. The association currently represents over sixty member organisations and acts as a national pressure group and a focus for liaison between members. It encourages the improvement of research techniques and devises guidelines and codes of practice. A mining history conference is held every two years.

For more details of local mining history societies or to obtain copies of NAMHO's codes of practice, please contact: The Secretary, NAMHO, c/o Peak District Mining Museum, The Pavilion, South Parade, Matlock Bath, Derbyshire, DE4 3NJ.

NAMHO wishes to emphasise that old mines are potentially dangerous and should not be explored underground without an experienced guide. Permission should always be obtained before venturing onto private property and the mention of a particular site does not imply any right of access.

IMAGES
of England

THE
EAST SHROPSHIRE
COALFIELDS

Compiled by
Ivor J. Brown

To my wife, Iris

TEMPUS

Tempus Publishing Limited
The Mill, Brimscombe Port,
Stroud, Gloucestershire, GL5 2QG

ISBN 0 7524 1705 3

Typesetting and origination by
Tempus Publishing Limited
Printed in Great Britain by
Midway Clark Printing, Wiltshire

The old ironstone waste tips at Finger Road, Dawley, c.1910. These tips form a backdrop to the community. Finger Road Chapel (now demolished) is on the left. The mounds of Portley, Paddock and Langley Fields pits, for which the abandonment plans were presented to the Inspector of Mines by the Coalbrookdale Company in the 1880s, were planted in part by unemployed men on 'credit note' schemes in the 1930s and more recently under reclamation schemes. They now form pleasant wooded hills.

Contents

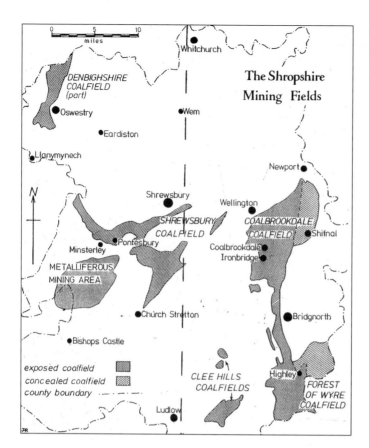

The Shropshire Mining Fields. The area covered by this book is shown on the right-hand half of this map.

Acknowledgements

This collection of photographs is the result of forty-five years work and, over this time, so many people have been involved it would be impossible to name them all. But to everyone with whom I have been in contact, as local residents, local historians or officers of organizations or groups, I give my thanks.

In particular I would like to thank the Ironbridge Gorge Museum – especially S.B. Smith, B.S. Trinder and J. Powell – the Shropshire Record Office and its officers over the years and the officers of the former Telford Development Corporation and the National Coal Board. The private mine owners and the members of the still thriving Shropshire Caving and Mining Club also deserve a mention, for without their help the underground visits necessary to obtain some of the pictures would not have been possible.

Old Shropshire miners and their families have been most helpful, particularly R. Blower and R. Rushton, as have many others, some of whom have passed away. Thanks are due to all who have provided photographs and illustrations, acknowledgement for which are made beneath their respective contributions. Photographs not credited are from the author's collection.

A special word of appreciation must be given to my wife, Iris, who for thirty-five years has typed, checked and given encouragement throughout the preparation of this and over 100 published papers on Shropshire mining.

Introduction

Shropshire is rich in the variety of minerals available. These range from the ores of the metals lead, zinc, copper and iron, to the fuels coal, oil and peat. A large number of general industrial and building materials are also available including 'red', 'brick' and 'tile' clays, fireclays, limestone, barytes, pyrites, calcite, salt, sand and sandstone. Igneous and metamorphic rocks suitable for use as aggregates are also available and are still being quarried. This publication, however, is concerned only with the underground extraction of minerals in the coalfields and while many historic photos of quarrying, open-casting and ore-mining exist these are not included in this work.

The map opposite shows the five distinct coalfields found within the county's limits. The Coalbrookdale Coalfield is by far the most important historically and economically. The Forest of Wyre Coalfield, the small and isolated Clee Hills Coalfield and the Shrewsbury Coalfield are all interesting but have contained few significant or medium-sized mines. Finally, around Oswestry, part of the Denbighshire Coalfield runs into the county, although it has always been more closely associated with industry in North Wales rather than the English Midlands.

Unusually, limestone has also been mined within or immediately adjoining the coalfield areas. This was possible due to geological unconformities in the strata, bringing the Carboniferous and Silurian limestones into contact with the coal measures. Limestone mines have existed at Ironbridge, near the Wrekin, at Lilleshall and at Novers and Gorstley Rough in the south of the county.

The mining industry of the Shropshire coalfields was never as large as in some other counties. It was significant, however, and reached its peak of importance early, due mainly to the many innovations with which it was associated. There is good evidence to indicate that the Romans used coal here and workings were recorded for ironstone and coal in the thirteenth and fourteenth centuries. By the seventeenth they formed an important industry. In the 1850s there were nearly 7,000 people employed producing over 1 million tons of coal and about 400, 000 tons of ironstone annually, albeit mainly from the Coalbrookdale field. This increased until in the 1870s, the peak years, more than 7,000 men and 1,000 women and girls were producing over 1.3 million tons of coal and 600,000 tons of ironstone annually.

Shropshire's share of the total British production then began to fall as other areas developed so that by 1900 Shropshire's eighty-eight mines produced just 780,420 tons of coal, 26,133 tons of ironstone, 14,996 tons of fireclay, 71,544 tons of red clay and 372 tons of pyrites. Employment was down to 2,848 men underground with 773 men and 125 women on the surface.

After 1900 the industry was fairly static for some time, employing around 3,800 people, although the number of women fell dramatically as less ironstone was produced. By the early 1920s about 4,000 men and less than ten females were employed. From this time employment fell slowly, with a slight rise later following mechanisation of the larger mines. The actual numbers were around 2,500 in 1938, 3,000 in 1948, 2,300 in 1968 and zero after the closure of Granville Colliery in 1979. Ironstone production had fallen to less than 200 tons per annum by 1921 and never rose again, finally dying out in the Second World War. The clay industry has held up, however, even into the present time – albeit from surface workings rather than underground.

The number of underground mines operating fell continuously from eighty-eight in 1900 until, at the date of nationalization of the coal industry in 1947, nine mines were nationalized, fourteen more became licensed mines and six clay mines were in private operation. All the mines were in the Coalbrookdale Coalfield except for one nationalized large mine in each of the Forest of Wyre and the Oswestry coalfields and one small mine in the Shrewsbury Coalfield.

About 50% of the photographs in this book were previously reproduced in the author's *Mines of Shropshire* (Moorland Publishing 1976) but this is long out of print and second-hand copies are now much in demand. The old photographs turned up in many different and some most unexpected places. One thing was common, however, and that was the thrill of identifying a long-lost view of Shropshire's industrial past. How many more old pictures lie hidden in drawers and cupboards it is impossible to guess, but it is certain that once these examples are seen others will be remembered and brought to light. Both the writer and the Ironbridge Gorge Museum would greatly like to know of any such find and perhaps a further volume can be prepared. It is certain that long-forgotten names will spring to mind as faces are recognized and incidents recalled. The writer would like to know of these too. As so much has depended on human memory it is quite possible that some of the detail may not be as accurate as that obtained purely from documentary sources. Every care has been taken to cross check the information given, but if anything is wrong the writer takes full responsibility.

The writer hopes that these pictures will give as much pleasure to others as they have given to him. Life and places are changing fast and only by studying contemporary scenes is it possible to understand fully the way of life of past generations. This way of life is being lost as the new town of Telford with new industries develops within the county, but fortunately a Museum Trust was set up thirty years ago with ideals which would ensure that some features would remain to give meaning to the pictures given here. The Ironbridge Gorge Museum Trust Ltd, a private charity, was established in 1968 to preserve the industrial heritage of the Coalbrookdale Coalfield. Wherever possible, relics have been preserved on site but the very situation of mining remains – deep underground or above dangerous mine shafts – in many cases precludes this possibility. Some items have therefore been taken to the Blists Hill Open Air Museum where they can be seen alongside reconstructed original remains, such as the Blists Hill Pit and steam winder, and replica mining items such as the drift mine. It is hoped that readers of this book will visit the museum, as only by a comparison of the physical remains with the documentary evidence can true understanding be achieved.

The grid reference number of most of the sites is given in the mines' index to enable the exact location to be identified on the local Ordnance Survey maps, copies of which would be useful to the reader in locating the former mine sites now that so much on the surface has changed.

A collection of lamps used at Shropshire mines. In 1907 the following flame safety lamps were in use for lighting and gas testing at Shropshire mines: 139 Marsaut, 162 Ackroyd & Best, 12 Cambrian, 374 Protector, 279 Mueseler and one Clanny. By the 1920s the larger mines were electrically lit but flame safety lamps continued to be used for gas detection until final closures. Candles were used at the Rock Fireclay Mine until it closed in 1964 and carbide acetylene lights were used at the private Shortwood Mine until the 1970s.

One

The Coalbrookdale Coalfield

This coalfield has been the most productive of the Shropshire fields. There is evidence to indicate that coal and ironstone were being worked throughout the Middle Ages and coal was certainly being used by the Romans long before this. It was, however, the successful substitution of coke for charcoal in the blast furnace by Abraham Darby in 1709 that led to the great expansion in mineral working in the area and ultimately to Coalbrookdale being dubbed the 'cradle of the Industrial Revolution'. It is often overlooked, however, that, prior to Darby's innovation, the prime mineral in the area had been ironstone and this mineral remained important until the end of the nineteenth century.

The minerals of the coalfield are found in the following geological series: the Upper Coal Measures, containing high quality red clays but poor coal-seams; the Middle and Lower Coal Measures, containing all the valuable seams of ironstone, coal and fireclay;

Miners at the Foxholes, Benthall, c.1916. Mining is unusual in that all technological levels can exist simultaneously. Here, even in the twentieth century, some miners prepare to dig coal in the outcrops and shallow deposits in Benthall Wood with simple tools. At a time of difficulty the landlord, in this case Lord Forester, was permitting some work on his land. At the rear left a miner is filling a bag of coal from a shallow deposit.

Carboniferous Limestone, containing the limestone worked at The Hatch, Steeraways and Lilleshall; and Silurian Limestone, lying unconformably beneath the Lower Coal Measures and mined in the area of Lincoln Hill.

For the miner and geologist the coalfield has posed many problems. These include numerous faults, folds and unconformities and an undulating topography, producing many seam outcrops. Other problems required special machinery and techniques, such as mine drainage, the gassy nature of the seams, their general thinness (on average about 3ft) and their variation in dip.

The proven coalfield is roughly rectangular in shape, about 7 miles by 3.5 miles and about 24 square miles in area. At its peak in the 1870s it produced over a million tons of coal per year and nearly half a million tons of ironstone, but ironstone production had reduced to a few hundred tons per year by 1914. The known statistics for clay are not so reliable but in 1896 underground mines produced 13,000 tons of fireclay and 57,000 tons of red clay while more was produced from surface operations. The production of clay continued to increase this century, mainly from open-casts and quarries, and remained at 250,000 tons annually until fairly recently.

Details of many aspects of mining are plentiful in government reports. For example, in the 1850s there were reportedly fifty-nine collieries, some made up of a number of mines, and the principal owners were: W.O. Foster (mines at Broseley, Ironbridge, Madeley Court); Coalbrookdale Company (Donnington Dawley, Horsehay, Lawley, Lightmoor); Lilleshall Company (Donnington, Wombridge, Priorslee, Wrockwardine Wood); Reynolds & Anstice or Madeley Wood Company (Madeley Wood, Madeley) and Beriah Botfield (Dark Lane, Hinkshay, Malinslee & Stirchley, Old Park and mines in the Clee Hill Coalfield). The Ketley Company was also important.

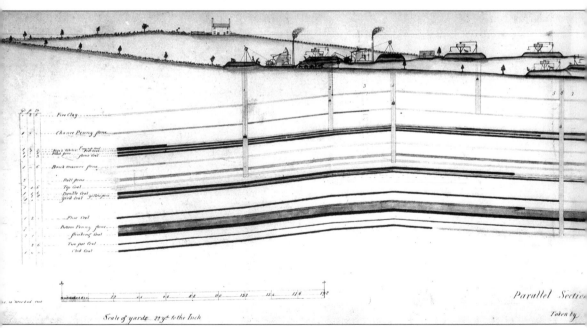

'Parallel Section of Hadley Colliery' by Charles W. Pearce, 1812. This is the earliest known illustrated geological section of a mine in the coalfield. It shows that ten seams of coal, seven of ironstone and one of fireclay were being worked at this time in strata aggregating 300ft thickness. The shafts were up to 400ft deep and the mine equipment included seven horse gins,

By 1891, at a time when ironstone production was fast declining, there were some eighty-seven pits in the coalfield of which twenty were clay mines, twelve were ironstone mines (although some coal was also produced at stone mines), and the rest were 'coal mines'.

In Shropshire terminology a colliery was a group of producing units, each called a pit or, more generally, a mine, under one manager. It did not matter whether the units produced coal, ironstone or clay. For example, Kemberton Pit (or Mine) and Halesfield Pit (or Mine) which had worked coal, ironstone and clay were in later years both part of Madeley Wood Colliery. In 1947 there were six collieries in the coalfield large enough to be nationalized: Kemberton (including Halesfield), Grange, Granville, Princes End (including Station 1 and 2 pits), Lawley (including Arleston, Lawley 3 and 4 pits and Lawley Drifts) and Old Park (Harris' pits). In addition there were thirteen small mines employing less than thirty men each, which became 'licensed mines'. There were also six privately owned clay mines unaffected by nationalization.

By the 1960s there were four mines left: the Rock Fireclay Mine, which closed in 1964, Madeley Wood Colliery (including Kemberton & Halesfield Pits), which closed in 1967, the Shortwoods Licensed Mine, which closed in 1970, and the last survivor, the Lilleshall Colliery (including Granville and Grange Pits), which closed in 1979. Coal and clay has, however, continued to be worked by open-cast means.

As a result of the intensive industrialisation of the area in the eighteenth and nineteenth centuries and its subsequent demise, much derelict land remained. Many of the scars have since been removed during land reclamation work for the construction of Telford New Town. Some former tips, however, have become wooded and still remain as a memorial to the efforts of the miners of the past.

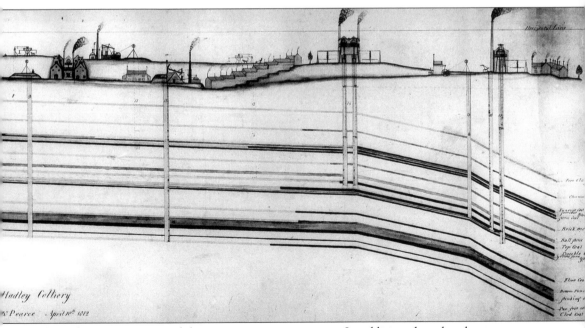

four whimsey engines and five steam pumping engines. In addition three hand capstan-type winders were in use, probably to assist with shaft repairs. It has been estimated that by 1800 there were over 200 steam engines at work in the coalfield, certainly more per square mile than in any other part of Britain at that time. (Apley Estates)

Innovations in mining

For its size the area is unique due to the number of innovations associated with it. These innovations included the formalised study of geological sections, the terminology for the system of access and for methods of working, the use of iron tramways and gravity inclines and of chains for winding and the extensive use and manufacture of steam engines. Many of these innovations can be seen applied in the photographs that follow.

Sections of strata

The interesting geology of the area attracted early and important geologists who often encouraged owners and miners to collect specimens of rock and fossils to draw up strata profiles as they sank their shafts. Imaginative names were given to their findings and charts were made of the successions. Some were illustrated, as in the Hadley section and in the scrolls drawn up later by the major companies. It is from the head of these scrolls that some of the following illustrations were taken.

The workable seams of ironstone, coal and fireclay are all found in less than 300ft of vertical strata and usually, at any one place, there were no more than seventeen workable seams of coal, seven of ironstone and three of fireclay. Only to the north of the coalfield are all the seams present. Toward the south the number falls until, around parts of Broseley, only the lowest is present, the others having been lost by erosion and geological unconformity. The red clays lie above the coal measures while the limestones, where present, lie beneath.

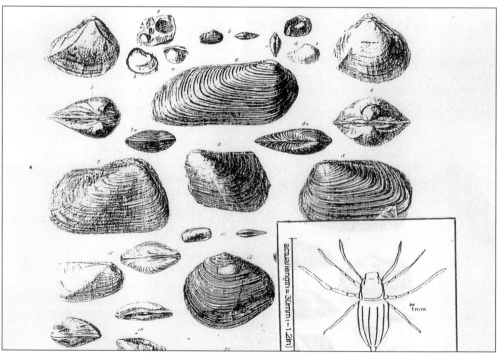

Fossils from the Coalbrookdale Coalfield. John Prestwich produced an important work in 1840 entitled 'On the Geology of Coalbrookdale'. This contains several pages illustrating local fossils, many from the collections of local ironmasters William Reynolds and John Anstice. Reynolds had encouraged the local miners to collect for him and paid them for their finds. The Anstices continued with their collection of both fossils and minerals. At least one of the fossils was named after the Anstices and it is still the subject of study.

Inset: The fossil 'Curculiodes ansticii', Buckland, 1837. This sketch is based on a paper by P.A. Selden in the Transactions of the Royal Society of Edinburgh, Earth Sciences, volume 83, published 1992.

NEW HADLEY.

1.	Earth and clay	2	0	0
2.	Wild red ground	23	2	0
3.	Bibley rock	0	2	0
4.	Strong red ground	6	2	0
5.	Four-feet rock	1	1	6
6.	Rock binds	0	2	0
7.	Strong clunch	1	2	0
8.	Penneystone rock	0	2	1
9.	Chance penneystone	1	0	0
10.	Clunch binds	0	3	0
11.	Coal and bass	0	1	6
12.	Fungous coal rock	9	0	0
13.	Fungous coal	1	0	0
14.	Poundstone and ragged robins	0	2	6
15.	Foot coal	0	1	0
16.	Clod	0	2	0
17.	Blackstone measure	1	0	6
18.	Clod and stone measure	1	1	6
19.	Soft fire clay	0	1	0
20.	Clod and gur coal	0	2	0
21.	Grey rock	7	0	0
22.	Brick-measure stone	1	0	6
23.	Clunch	1	0	0
24.	Bind	0	2	0
25.	Bass	0	2	0
26.	Bind rock	8	0	0
27.	Ballstone	2	0	0
28.	Dun earth	2	2	0
29.	Top coal	1	1	6
30.	Slums and three-quarter coal	0	2	6
31.	Double coal rock	3	0	0
32.	Double coal	1	0	0
33.	Double coal bottoms	0	1	6
34.	Poundstone	0	2	0
35.	Yellow stone	0	2	6
36.	Bass	0	1	0
37.	Yard coal and bass	1	0	0
38.	Clod	0	2	6
39.	Pitcher bass	1	2	0
40.	Eight-yard rock	8	0	0
41.	Strong rock binds	4	2	0
42.	Flint coal	1	2	0
43.	Flint coal rock	6	0	0
44.	Bottom penneystone	7	0	0
45.	Sulphur coal	2	1	0
46.	Gritty fire clay	2	0	0
47.	Coal bass and coal	1	2	6
48.	Clunch	2	1	0
49.	Two feet coal	0	2	6
50.	Clunch	1	2	0
51.	Coal and bass	0	0	6
52.	Clunch binds	2	0	6
53.	Clod coal	1	0	0
54.	White and blue clunch	7	0	0
55.	Little flint coal	0	1	6
56.	White rock	3	0	0
57.	Crawstone fee (or measure,)	0	2	3
		142	2	4

PIT IN EDWARD'S PIECE, HADLEY.

1.	Cat brain	24	0	0
2.	Essbull rock	10	0	0
3.	Four-foot coal	2	0	0
4.	Brown clod	1	1	0
5.	Black clod or clunch	4	2	0
6.	Coal	0	0	9
7.	Funker's rock	8	0	0
8.	Bass	0	0	6
9.	Funker's coal	1	0	3
10.	Funker's coal poundstone	0	2	0
11.	Bass	0	2	0
12.	Two foot coal	0	2	0
13.	Blackstone measure	1	2	0
14.	Stone coal	0	2	8
15.	Clunch or slums	2	0	0
16.	Gur coal	0	1	0
17.	Clunch	6	0	0
18.	Grey rock	3	2	0
19.	Brick measure	2	1	0
20.	Bind bass	1	0	3
21.	Bind	7	1	0
22.	Ballstone clod	4	0	0
23.	Top coal bass	0	1	0
24.	Top coal	1	1	6
25.	Slum	1	0	0
26.	Double coal rock	2	1	6
27.	Double coal	0	2	10
		98	0	3

NEW HADLEY.

Sandstone & conglomerate.
Red Marl
Sandstone
Arenaceous Shale.
Sandstone.
Argillaceous Shale
COAL & UNDERCLAY
Hard Sandstone.
FUNGUS.
COAL 1 FT. 0 INS.
UNDERCLAY with 'black' Ironstone.
COAL 1 FT. 0 INS. & UNDERCLAY.
Hard grey Sandstone.
Argillaceous Shale & 'Brick' Ironstone.
Carbonaceous Shale.
Hard Arenaceous Shale.
Argillaceous Shale & nodules of Ironstone.
'TOP' COAL 7 FT. 0 INS.
SILICIFEROUS UNDERCLAY.
'DOUBLE' COAL 4 FT. 6 INS.
UNDERCLAY & Carbonaceous Shale.
'YARD' COAL 3 FT. 0 INS.
UNDERCLAY & Carbonaceous Shale
Hard grey Sandstone.
Arenaceous Shale.
'BIG FLINT' COAL 5 FT. 0 INS.
Hard Sandstone.
Argillaceous Shale & 'penny' Ironstone fossiliferous.
'SULPHUR' COAL 7 FT. 0 INS.
FIRECLAY.
COAL 5 FT. 6 INS.
UNDERCLAY
COAL 2 FT. 6 INS.
COAL 0 FT. 6 INS. & UNDERCLAY.
'CLOD' COAL 3 FT. 0 INS.
GREY UNDERCLAY
'LITTLE FLINT' COAL 1 FT. 6 INS.
WHITE SILICIFEROUS UNDERCLAY.
Arenaceous Shale.
Farewell Rock.

146 yd 2 ft 0 in (approx)

Shaft sections from the Coalbrookdale Coalfield, 1840 and 1846. These are similar to the shaft sections shown on the Hadley Colliery section on pages 10 and 11. The one to the left is from John Prestwich's 1840 collection of twenty-nine sections of the coalfield. Some of his sections dated back to the eighteenth century. In 1846 John Williams also collected and published a number of sections in chart form. The Hadley section is shown. The word 'stone' meant ironstone to local miners and the word 'clunch' often meant fireclay.

An engraving of a specimen of the fossil tree 'Sigillaria'. This was discovered in a quarry at Coalbrookdale in 1863. Numerous similar specimens have been found in the Big Flint sandstone of the area. This sandstone forms the roof of the Pennystone ironstone seam, the most productive ironstone measure in the coalfield. Similar specimens have also been found in the Little Flint sandstone at the base of the productive measures. (*Illustrated London News*, 7 February 1863)

'Seeking coal at the Black Rock, Coalbrookdale', 1912. It is probable that the striking miners were looking for the Little Flint coal-seam at its outcrop, since 'Black Rock' is the local name for the sandstone roof of this seam, derived from its heavy impregnation with bitumen. (D. Oakley)

Access to mines

A stratified material such as coal, ironstone, fireclay or limestone can be accessed in three ways, and for each of these the Shropshire miner developed his own terminology:

1. Cropping – working from the outcrop where it lies at shallow depth, removing the overburden or 'deadrock', a method now called open-casting or quarrying. In recent years open-casting has played a major part in removing the mining scars around Ketley, Lawley, Old Park and Clares Lane.

2. Insetting using day levels – once known as 'footrids' or 'footridges', but nowadays called adits – where tunnels are driven into the outcrop of a seam or into the bank until a seam is reached. These are numerous along both banks of the Ironbridge Gorge and in the upland parts of the coalfield around Broseley, Lightmoor and Wrockwardine Wood. A 'sow' or 'sough' was an adit used for drainage.

3. 'Daypits', 'dayholes' or shafts, where a well or pit was sunk down to the seams. These often worked in conjunction with adits, assisting the ventilation and drainage of the underground workings.

The steep sided Ironbridge Gorge that cuts across the coalfield had many 'insetts', or adits, driven into it from the earliest times, while cropping took place on the bank tops. The early shafts constructed in those positions, often with primitive equipment, have also been illustrated by many important visitors to the Gorge.

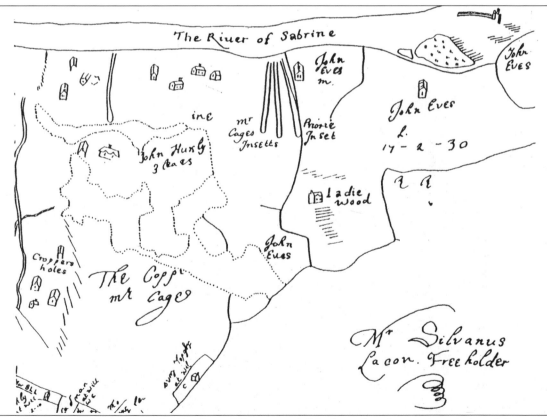

Part of 'The Plott of Broseley' by Samuel Parsons, c.1621, the earliest known 'mine' plan of the area, showing 'croppers holes' and 'insetts'. This is a tracing from a plan in Shropshire Record Office, No.1224/1/32. (C. Clark)

'A view of Lincoln Hill with the Ironbridge in the distance taken from the side of the River Severn', 1788. This engraving by James Fittler (1758-1835) after George Robertson (1724-1788), published by J. and J. Boydell, London, appears to show the loading of coal lumps and slack into Severn trows for transportation down the river, possibly to Worcester and Gloucester. The River Severn was the main means of communication between the coalfield and the outside world up to the early years of the nineteenth century. (Ironbridge Gorge Museum)

'Lateral mine shafts beside the Severn'. The drawing was published by Dibden (1745-1814) in 1801. At this time Dibden produced an interesting account of the Tar Tunnel and it is possible that one of these 'lateral mine shafts' or adits represents the mouth of this tunnel. The picture shows a similar tunnel on the opposite river bank but there is no geological or historical evidence for such a tunnel. It is more likely therefore that the caverns shown were in fact lime kilns at Lincoln Hill and Benthall respectively and that the pyramid of light above the tunnel represents the flames from the kiln. (See the view of the lime kilns at Coalbrookdale by J.M.W. Turner, published in 1825, for a similar lighting effect.). (Morley Tonkin Collection)

16

'The Great Wheel at Broseley', c.1802, a sepia-tinted drawing by Paul Sandby Munn (1773-1845) Although the waterwheel, the subject of the drawing, was not connected with mining, the background shows clearly a horse gin at a shaft mine in Benthall Wood. The mine was one of a great number to be worked in this vicinity; indeed a small adit mine for coal and clay was at work less than 50yds from the wheel site as recently as 1952. This is one of a number of early views of horse gins used in the coalfield. The wheel was used for driving a mill, at first used as an oil and colour mill then later as a corn mill, but similar wheels, though smaller, have been used for driving pumps within the Shropshire coalfields. (Elton Collection)

'A view of the mouth of a coal pit near Broseley'. This print was published in 1788, the artist being George Robertson (c.1724-1788) and the engraver, Francis Chesham. The gin seems to be powered by two horses, which would indicate that the mine was fairly deep. This is also borne out by the fact that a surface-furnace ventilating system was in use. The chimney from the furnace is shown on the right of the picture. Horses with panniers for transportation can be seen in the foreground. (Ironbridge Gorge Museum)

Methods of working

Having accessed the seam, a method of working had to be devised. Traditionally, early workings were in the form of a widening in the seam called a 'bell' but this needed thick seams with strong roofs to be successful. This was not a common situation in the coalfield but bellpitting was used around Lawley and parts of Broseley. The other traditional method was 'pillar and stall', where workings were opened out by tunnelling in a checkerboard fashion, leaving pillars to support the roof. Many shallow mines used this method but it was not safe at depth as the roof weight could crush the pillars and it was also difficult to prevent leakage when 'coursing' air through a gassy mine like those in Shropshire. The Shortwoods Mine and other shallow mines, however, used this method until they closed.

Shropshire is said to have developed another method in the seventeenth century which overcame the above problems. It soon became known as Shropshire 'Long Work' or 'Long Wall'. Originally the method developed from extending the stalls in a pillar working and gradually opening the face as work proceeded (see figures). At first all the miners would have to enter the face from the roadway together, and fill their boxes, dans or tubs simultaneously (known as 'tubstall' working) but later the face was straightened so that a 'conveyor' path could be left behind the advancing miners. Nearly all major British deep mines have used this method in recent years

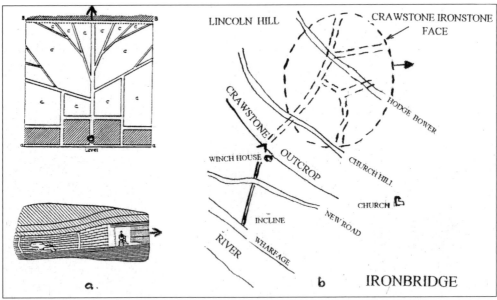

The Shropshire Long Wall method. Figure 'a' shows in diagrammatic form how the area around the shaft was 'blocked out' in pillar and stall fashion which later developed into long-wall working, seen in this case with a straight 'face' (B – B), the arrow showing the direction of advance. (From Ure's *Dictionary of Arts* by R. Hunt, 1878, and *Annals of Coal Mining* by R.L. Galloway, 1898). Figure 'b' shows a sketch of a long-wall face completely encircling the workings from a single entrance in an early nineteenth century Crawstone Ironstone mine at Ironbridge, as explored in 1974. The arrow again shows the direction of advance.

'The Shropshire Method of 'Long Work'', 1860. This illustration from *The Playbook of Metals* by J.H. Pepper shows Shropshire miners working on a long-wall face of unusual thickness. The roof supports and means of removing the mineral have been omitted for clarity and effect. (R.Vernon)

A view of a part of a long-wall face worked in the early nineteenth century in the thin Crawstone ironstone seam at Ironbridge. The iron-bearing sandstone on which the hammer rests is about 2ft thick. Below it is a 6in-thick seam of coal which was removed first to allow the ironstone to fall and break for removal. The roof is of a harder sandstone, 'flintstone', with many well-formed fossilised tree roots. The photograph was taken in 1974.

'Tramways' (waggonways or railroads) and gravity inclines

These can be seen on local maps of the seventeenth and eighteenth centuries. Many were among the earliest known in Britain. The earliest were made of wood but from the 1700s iron was used. The hilly nature of the southern part of the area led to the development of 'gravity inclines', straight runs where trucks going downhill could pull empty ones uphill using rope or chains or alternatively, loaded trucks went down under gravity and were hauled back by hand or other means. These were used underground as well as on the surface as late as the early years of the twentieth century. Similar inclines were used locally with carriages carrying boats between high-level and low-level canals.

Winding from shafts

Ordinary rope and single link chain has been used for centuries but with deeper shafts and heavier loads something stronger was required. During the latter years of the eighteenth century local ironfounders began to improve the type of chains used. By 1807 Gilbert Gilpin had added grooves to pulleys. Botfields of Shifnal began improving the metals used for chain construction and Edge of Coalport redesigned the chains and put them side by side, pinning them together across the flats with oak pins to create twin- and later triple-link chains. James Edge, the founder's son, received a prize for them at the 1851 Great Exhibition. From this time the Coalbrookdale Coalfield was foremost in the production of these 'safety chains' and, even when superseded generally by wire ropes, they continued in use at a few mines in the coalfield until about 1920. The equipment used with flat chain lent itself to being used with flat wire rope, in which several wire ropes were 'stitched' together to form one flat rope, and the larger collieries changed to these. Flat wire ropes were last used in Shropshire and North East England in the 1950s (see photographs of Grange Mine, page 73).

A gravity incline at 'Tykes Nest', Broseley, early nineteenth century The inclines on the southern bank of the Ironbridge Gorge conveyed coal, ironstone, clay and limestone down to the river. This view seems to show the quarrying and transport of limestone. It is from an album of sketches by Joseph Banks (c.1780-1835).

An incline winding house at a Crawstone ironstone mine in 1995. This almost-circular building stands at the top of a steep path, almost certainly a former incline (shown on the map on page 18). It is immediately alongside the entrance adit to old ironstone workings and probably dates to about 1800, possibly earlier.

Left: An advertisement by Edge & Sons of Shifnal, 1893. Edge & Sons sold both chains and ropes for mines at this time and were eventually taken over by British Ropes Ltd. Established in the late 1700s, the company finally closed down in 1971. (*Colliery Managers' Pocket Book*, 1893)

Right: A length of triple-link winding chain, c.1861. This photograph was taken by George Maw, whose company was an important clay and clay products manufacturer in the area. The three chains are pinned together through the flats by oak pegs. (Ironbridge Gorge Museum)

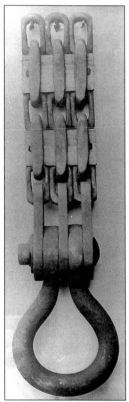

A Coalbrookdale Company hydraulic engine, 1819. This hydraulic pressure engine was found at a depth of 360ft in a shaft known as the Wills Founder at Winster, in the lead mining area of Derbyshire. It was raised to the surface in 1976 by members of the Peak District Mines Historical Society and, having been restored, is now in the Peak District Mining Museum at Matlock Bath. The pressure to operate the engine came not from steam but from water in a column in the shaft. The nameplate, bearing the legend 'Coalbrookdale 1819', is shown on the crosspiece towards the left. (Peak District Mining Museum)

Two

The Coalbrookdale Company

Mining in the Ironbridge Gorge predates even the arrival of Abraham Darby I who founded the Coalbrookdale Company in 1708. Darby took over a pre-existing furnace but his early successful substitution of coke for charcoal in smelting soon led to a great increase in both ironstone and coal production. The company's principal mines were in Broseley, Lawley, New Works, Dawley and Horsehay and many of these mines had steam engines and pumps built at the Company's own works. The Company also introduced iron rails and built the now world-famous Iron Bridge. In the eighteenth century the Company also operated some works which later became part of the operations of the Madeley Wood Company and the Ketley Company.

The Coalbrookdale Company was, in its day, a major mine operator. In 1837, for example, it had thirty-one ironstone pits producing about 4,200 tons of stone per month from the Twopenny, Blue Flat, White Flat, Ballstone and Spar seams. Many of the pit mounds around Horsehay, Lawley, Lightmoor and Dawley were produced by them at this time (p.5). Their last blast furnaces, at Lightmoor and Dawley Castle, were blown out by 1890.

Unfortunately, few photographs exist of the Company's own mining operations as they had largely withdrawn from these by the late nineteenth century but they did continue mining clay and some coal to the 1930s. In 1891 the Company operated four coal mines, at Brandlee, Fair View, Heath Hill and Ladygrove, and two clay mines, at Cherry Tree Hill and Dell Hole. By 1908 they operated only Gravel Leasow and Lower Lightmoor Clay Pits. In the 1920s they worked the Best and Two Foot coal and red clay mines at Jubbs Leasow and occasionally other small mines finishing at Lightmoor in around 1935. These later mines supplied the clay for brick-making and, later, firebricks and roofing tiles, at Shutfield and Lightmoor Works. The Coalbrookdale Company Works is still in operation although its form and products have changed.

Roasting in kilns, Coalbrookdale, c.1850. When the ironstone nodules or lumps had been collected at the mine surface the stone had to be upgraded by removal of some of the impurities. This could be done in open heaps or in kilns. This view of the type of kilns used is taken from Charles Tomlinson's *Cyclopaedia of Useful Arts*, 1852-1854.

A Newcomen-type steam winding engine at Lightmoor in around 1860. The engine is believed to have been made by the Coalbrookdale Company for its own mine, the Gravel Leasow. Of particular interest is the reel-type winding drum used with a winding chain. In 1837 the Company is said to have been working eighty-one ironstone mines of this type, producing about 4,200 tons of ironstone per month. Nearly all of these had closed by 1890. (Ironbridge Gorge Museum)

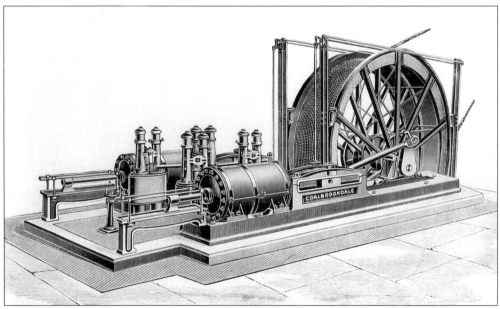

A Coalbrookdale Company winding engine, 1902. This photograph is taken from an illustration in the Company's 1902 catalogue. The Company is much less known for its winding than for its pumping engines and none of the Company's winding engines are known to have been preserved. (Ironbridge Gorge Museum)

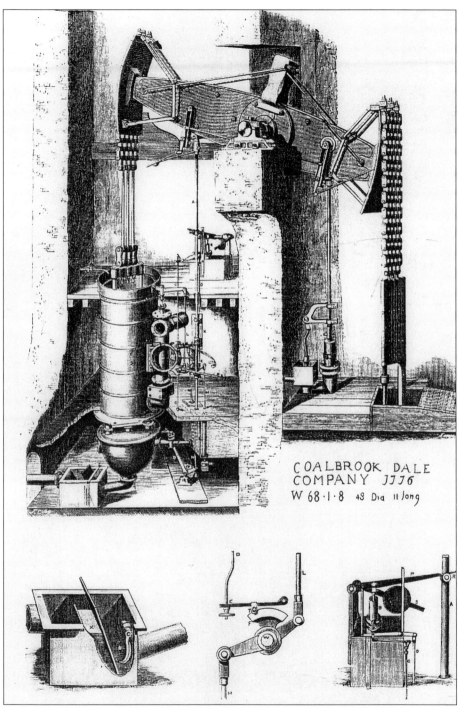

COALBROOK DALE
COMPANY 1776
W 68·1·8 48 Dia 11 long

An early Newcomen-type pumping engine built by the Coalbrookdale Company in 1776. This engine is said to have been used at Old Handley Wood Pit, Shropshire, and transferred to a pit at Staveley near Chesterfield in 1849. The site of Handley Wood is not known but there is a 'Handleys Hitch' at Broseley or it could be Hadley Wood near Donnington. (*The Engineer*, 1880)

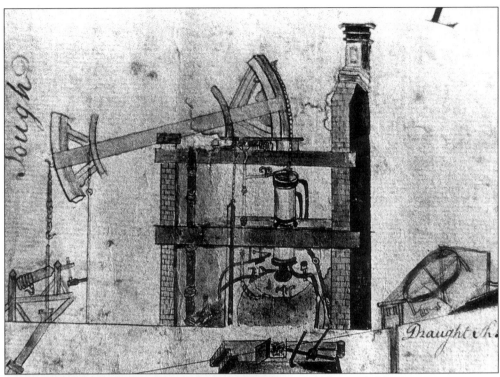

Another early Newcomen-type pumping engine, 1760. This drawing, from the 'Plan of Millclose Works in Cowley Knowle 1760' by W. Dawson, is in the Ironbridge Gorge Museum Collection. It shows an early engine believed to have been supplied by Abraham Darby of Coalbrookdale Works. As well as showing the engine and its house the drawing also depicts a hand winch (left) and the artist's impression of a horse gin (right). (Ironbridge Gorge Museum)

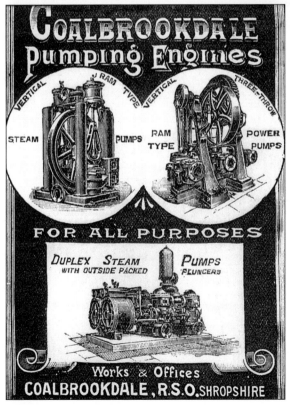

Coalbrookdale pumping engines, 1902. The company produced a wide range of engines over the years; this advertisement is from the *Colliery Managers' Pocket Book* of 1902. Hydraulically powered pumping engines were also produced and one, built in 1819 for the Alport Mines, Derbyshire, is now preserved in the Peak District Mining Museum at Matlock (see page 22).

THE SPRINGWELL PIT ACCIDENT,
LITTLE-DAWLEY, SHROPSHIRE.

On December 6th, 1872, at a few minutes past four pm, as eight unfortunate colliers were ascending the pit, the chain suddenly broke, precipating them 50 yards down the pit, and hurrying them into eternity.

Names: William Bailey, 21, Married. Edward Jones, 21, Single. Robert Smith, 18, Single. John Parker, 22, Single. Allen Wykes, 20, Single. Isaiah Skelton, 15, Single. John Yale, 21, Single. John Davies, 19, Single.

They were all interred in one vault, at the Parish Church, Dawley, on Tuesday, December 10th.

What a world of care and trouble,
Daily, nightly, we bewail;
The loss of father, brother, cousin,
Or some relative, ...sad's their tale.
Pelsall calamity scarcely o'er,
When awful news comes to our ears,
That eight poor colliers have departed
Out of this mournful vale of tears.

'Twas on the sixth day of December,
At Springwell Pit, sad to relate,
In Dawley Field, in brave old Shropshire,
Eight healthy men met their sad fate.
Their work being done, for home preparing,
And to the bottom they had come,
Little thinking their days were numbered,
And that they'd never see their home.

The band had started, eight ascending,
Cheerful as the noonday sun,
When, little thinking, for a moment,
Every man his race had run.
When, lo! a whirl that colliers call it,
Took its awful course, we're told,
And dashed the eight men to the bottom,
Smashed to atoms. But their souls ...

Were wafted, quick as lightning,
To their Maker, up on high;
Who gives us colliers daily warning,
That our end is very nigh.
We who toil and bravely labour,
Hard to earn our daily bread;
We cannot tell the day nor hour,
But what we may be brought home dead.

A fearful sight was at the bottom,
Men cut and bruised from head to toe;
With tons of chain and iron upon them,
Which filled the collier's hearts with woe.
But fear and danger at such a moment,
Never enters a collier's heart;
So they toiled with anxious labour,
In hope that some hurt, may have a spark

Of life within their mangled bodies,
To cheer them toiling down below;
But strength and hope had nearly vanished,
Only two could breathe, but lo,
Their prayers to God the only giver
Of life and health, were quickly raised;
That he had spared those few below,
To repent of sin and mend their ways.

So that at every moment,
They may stand for ever blest;
And always ready to meet danger,
To be sure of eternal rest.
So may Christ the loved Redeemer,
Fit each collier for above;
And unite each one as brother,
And turn all hatred into love.

So that all at the last trumpet,
Will be called to our Saviour's side,
Where all dangers and troubles ended,
For ever there with Christ to abide.
Where songs to God through eternity,
Mingle with the blest above;
May each collier feel the blessing,
With all strife turned into love.

May He bless the widowed mother,
And the offspring by her side;
May He crown the sorrowing mothers, -
Fathers, sisters, and brothers guide.
And each day give them grace and glory,
To guide their feet in paths of right;
That when their journey here is ended,
He'll take them to eternal light.

A 'disaster ballad' commemorating the Springwell Pit Accident of 1872. Ballads were published after most accidents involving more than two deaths. They were usually sold for one or two pence, the profit being donated to the dependants of the dead miners. This ballad was produced after a winding chain broke at one of the Coalbrookdale Company's mines. The miners who died were buried together in a common vault, which can still be seen in Dawley's Holy Trinity Churchyard. A similar vault can be seen at Madeley (see page 45).

A horse gin near Lightmoor, c.1937. This drawing is by J. Willocks, from a photograph which appeared in *Shropshire, the geography of the county* by W.W. Watts in 1939. The Lightmoor area was worked by the Coalbrookdale Company in the twentieth century, mainly for clay, and this is probably at one of their pits. The gin obviously had two chains or ropes moving in the shaft, one over each pulley, with one going down while the other went up. The narrow drum would indicate that it was in fact a single rope with just one wrapping round the drum. One end of the rope would carry the cage, the other the counterbalance weight.

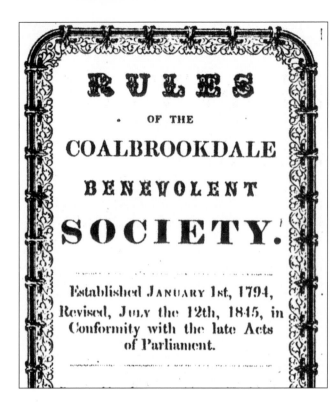

RULES

OF THE

COALBROOKDALE

BENEVOLENT

SOCIETY.

Established JANUARY 1st, 1794,
Revised, JULY the 12th, 1845, in
Conformity with the late Acts
of Parliament.

Rulebook of the Coalbrookdale Benevolent Society, 1845. Benevolent or friendly societies were a feature of the industrial area. They were set up to cater for some of the needs of workers who became sick, were injured or died at work. The Coalbrookdale Society, however, had a rule that 'no collier or miner shall be admitted a member: and any person entering, and afterwards going to work in the pits, shall thereupon cease being a member, and forfeit all his interest'. This was presumably because miners were considered too great a risk.

Iron Bridge.

A postcard showing the River Severn and the Iron Bridge, c.1900. Some of the local ironstone was used for local requirements – the Iron Bridge, the fence on the riverside, the local waggonways, cooking pots and fireplaces in the workers' houses – while some was exported using Severn trows, an example of which is shown moored at the river bank.

Three
The Madeley Wood Company

The Madeley Wood Company was really an offshoot from the Coalbrookdale Company and eventually took over its mining operations on the river bank and downstream. By 1900 it was, as a mining company in Shropshire, second only to the Lilleshall Company. It operated mines of coal, ironstone, fireclay, red clay and limestone as well as blast furnaces, brickworks and tileworks. The company owed its origins to Richard Reynolds, who married into the Darby family in 1757. At this time he took a one-third share of Ketley furnaces and mines and from 1763-1768 he managed the Coalbrookdale Company until Abraham Darby (the third) was old enough to take over himself. During this time Reynolds developed his own interests alongside those of the Coalbrookdale Company.

Richard Reynolds' interests passed to his sons William and Joseph and in 1796 they were separated from those of the Coalbrookdale Company. William concentrated on the Madeley Wood activities which included developing the 'new town'of Coalport, mining around Madeley Wood and the local transport systems – tramroads, canals, tunnels, tunnel-shaft systems and inclines.

When William died in 1803 a share of his estate passed to William Anstice, who for a while operated the company as Reynolds and Anstice, concentrating on the Madeley Wood operations. His son, John, took over in 1858, eventually acquiring the Reynolds' share too. For a while the company was called Anstice & Co. but eventually a long-standing unofficial title, Madeley Wood Company, became the official one. John Anstice's main contribution was a redevelopment at Halesfield Mine and the development of the new shafts at Kemberton Mine in the 1860s. At this time he was employing nearly 900 people. John provided well for his workers including a school and mission room and on his death his friends and employees built a large Memorial Hall to his memory at Madeley. The Anstices continued to own the company until the 1920s at which time one of the managers, John Cadman, bought it. The Cadman ownership continued until nationalization in 1947.

In 1891 the Company operated eight substantial mines but by 1908 only three large and two smaller ones remained. After the closure of Blists Hill Ironworks in 1912 contraction continued until market conditions for coal later improved. In 1947 the Company's surviving mine, the Kemberton Mine, was nationalized. It then expanded until over 800 people were employed but eventually closed in 1967.

Anstice Memorial Institute, Madeley, *c*.1900. This hall was built in memory of John Anstice as a community centre and 'Workmens' Club and Institute' within ten years of the first such hall being built in the country. The building was opened in 1870 but shortly after was severely damaged by fire. When reopened it provided rooms for games, concerts and lectures, a library, banking services and a restaurant, but political and religious meetings were forbidden (although this was changed later). The building survives, now crowded into the centre of a small, modern shopping complex.

Madeley Wood Hall, home of the Anstices, *c*.1900. The mine-owning Anstice family first lived at Bedlam Hall but this became affected by ground movement. They then moved to Madeley Wood Hall, one mile along the riverside. They were leading figures in the District, but found time for their workers. The local school logbook shows that their womenfolk worked as volunteers in the school and John Anstice is said to have cried openly with relatives after a mine fatality. In 1851 John Anstice employed six house servants and fifteen estate workers about his 100-acre farm, besides the 800 employees in the mines, brickyards and furnaces.

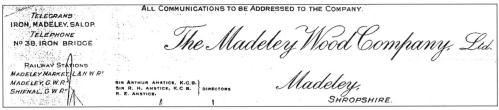

Madeley Wood Company letterhead, c.1920.

'Adams Engine' and ironstone pits, Madeley Wood, Shropshire, 1847. The artist, Warrington Smyth (1817-1890), became a mining geologist for the Geological Survey in 1844 and carried out some work for the Mines Inspectorate. His early years seem to have been spent mainly in the Shropshire area and he produced several sketches of the sites he had visited including this view of an ironstone mine at work. It was probably one of the mines at the Lloyds. The engine was obviously constructed at ground level and as the ironstone-bearing shale was drawn from the mine it was placed in layers around the shaft top. Women and girls, shown on the right, were then employed to pick out the ironstone nodules and place them into 'ranks', or heaps, for firing, which removed some of the impurities. (Ironbridge Gorge Museum)

Madeley Wood Iron Furnaces, 1847. A further drawing by Warrington Smyth which shows the Company's new iron furnaces. They are on a site now part of the Ironbridge Gorge Museum and known as Blists Hill. Some of the building remains can still be seen. (Ironbridge Gorge Museum)

31

A Madeley Wood Colliery engine, 1879. This engine could have been at almost any of the mines in the Madeley area. It is a Heslop beam winding and pumping engine. In 1878 an engine of this kind, believed to be the last of its type, was presented to the Patents Museum (now the Science Museum) in London. The notice of this donation in *The Times* of 24 May 1879 led to a letter from W.R. Anstice of the Madeley Wood Company saying that they 'still have three of the same description at work, they had five and once had eight'. The last of these engines ceased work in 1917. (Science Museum)

A Madeley Wood Colliery engine, c.1890. This engine, very similar but possibly not the same as the one above, was said to have been at the Lane Pit, Madeley (part of Brick Kiln Leasow Mine). This is a rear view showing the open-top cylinder. It is one of a set of photographs available of this engine, which was probably disused at this time.

Madeley Wood and the Lloyds, 1948. This is one of the oldest mining areas in Shropshire, with records going back to the 1600s. Madeley Wood community is at the bottom of the photograph. The area known as 'the Lloyds' is shown mainly as treeless spoil from the ironstone mines with the L-shaped group of cottages built for the Madeley Wood Company's workers in the early eighteenth century at top centre. There was a steam engine at the Lloyds in 1719 and several others followed including the large pumping engine over the page. All mining in this area had ceased by about 1910. (Cambridge University Collection)

The New Buildings at the Lloyds, 1968. These two rows were the homes of some of the local miners. They were demolished in the 1970s. Around the homes were the many mines, the pumping engine, workshops, offices, school and mission room. The view is from the southern bank of the river Severn, with the Severn Valley Railway and gatekeeper's cottage in the foreground. Both banks of the Ironbridge Gorge are at this point very unstable and subject to landslip. (R. Miles)

The Lloyds pumping engine, c.1900. This was a 'central' pumping engine used to drain several mines of this area. Some of the pits were sunk in the late eighteenth century and a steam engine is known to have been here by 1820 but was probably old at this time. The engine is shown on a plan of 1840. The pump's 'forks broke' in around 1911 and all works ceased the following year. An account of this mine describes the engine as having an open-top, 26in-diameter cylinder with an 8ft stroke. The cast-iron beam was 20ft long and the rods raised the water from a 300ft depth. The equipment was said to be 115 years old. The wooden rod or spear can be clearly seen with bulky timbers connecting the sections. To the left there is a capstan which would be used to raise or lower wooden rods during repair work. (R. Miles)

The Tar Tunnel, Coalport, 1970. One of the most unusual features about this coalfield is the presence of natural bitumen, or 'tar' as the local miners called it, in sufficient quantity to be exploited. This particular tunnel was being driven from the river bank to the mines in 1787 when a tar spring was tapped. The tar was subsequently collected in wells. Many famous people came to see this natural wonder. The tunnel eventually connected with the mine shafts after about 1,000yds and continued to be used for ventilation and drainage until the 1930s. It was then closed but was 'rediscovered' and surveyed in 1964.

A 'tar well' in the Tar Tunnel, 1970. The tar runs down the tunnel walls, exuding from the sandstone in cavities behind them. It was collected and held by clay dams until, when sufficient was present, the dams were breached and water carried the 'tar' to the tunnel entrance. The first 100yds of the tunnel are accessible today as part of the Ironbridge Gorge Museum. The tar is the shiny black substance on the walls and on the pool at the bottom of the photo.

During 1974 four miners were employed clearing out the Tar Tunnel using rails and side-tipping 'Jubilee' waggons. The waste material was temporarily stored in the canal basin at the foot of the Hay Incline, which was the inclined railway connection between the local tub boat canal and a short canal running parallel to the river Severn. This canal incline superseded the shaft-tunnel system of which the Tar Tunnel was to have been part.

Inside the 'conserved' Tar Tunnel, 1980, showing the recently installed railway, the lighting arrangements and, to the right, the forced draught ventilation system. The original 'tar drain' lies beneath the ventilation ducts. Only about one-tenth of the total length of tunnel has been conserved in this way. This is the section now open to the public.

Blists Hill Mine, *c*.1900. This mine was operated by the Madeley Wood Company until 1916 after which date it was sold to George Legge. It finally closed in 1940. The shafts were almost certainly sunk in the 1780s, eventually reaching a depth of 202yds. The minerals worked included five seams of coal, two of ironstone and two of fireclay. These were all worked before 1870, from which time the mine concentrated on two additional seams of red tile clay, worked from an inset about 127yds down the shafts. After 1870 the mine rarely employed more than twenty men. The picture shows the miners employed and the two ponies, Ben and Turpin. These ponies were raised and lowered through the shaft at this and the adjoining Shawfield Mine as required. The early engines were of the Heslop type but from 1912 a horizontal single-cylinder engine was used. This remained at the mine until 1956. (B. Waterson)

The Madeley Wood Company's Blists Hill furnaces, 1912. Compare this view with that on p.31. Most of the ironstone and some of the coal produced at the company's mines was used here. The coal was converted to coke nearby, as shown on p.40, and some limestone was brought from the company's Lincoln Hill Mines. The engine house on the left was rebuilt in 1873 with a different window style. The furnace closed during 1912 after an industrial dispute.

Blists Hill Mine, 1935. The photograph shows the cage at the shaft top. The small tub contained a load of hard red clay which had to be allowed to weather before it could be used. During weathering the clay was turned several times. In 1916 the mine was transferred to George Legge but all deep mining operations had ceased here by 1941. (F. Turner)

Blists Hill Mine, c.1940. The photograph shows the water pit and the means by which the mine was kept clear of water. A 'bowk' or 'kibble' was lowered into the sump, filled, raised to the surface and emptied into a wooden trough through which it passed into the nearby canal. (F. Turner)

Blists Hill Mine engine, 1980. The Blists Hill Mine surface has been reconstructed and is now part of the Ironbridge Gorge Museum. The engine house has been rebuilt and a steam winding engine dating from the 1860s installed. The engine is similar to the original and was obtained from the nearby Milburgh Clay Mine. It is in operation daily and at present winds from a depth of about 15yds in the original shaft. (Ironbridge Gorge Museum)

Blists Hill Mine engine house and boiler, 1995. A vertical boiler is used for steam raising of a style common to the area. The brick engine house is to the left of the picture. Beyond this is the shaft with a reconstructed head-frame.

The coke hearths, Blists Hill, c.1890. The mine headgear, engine house and haystack boiler can be seen in the background. In the foreground coal is being coked by stacking around small pillars, covering and partially firing. The coke was used in the adjoining blast furnaces. (B. Waterson)

Watering, weathering and turning clay, Blists Hill, c.1935. As the clay was very hard when first brought to surface it had to be weathered for three months before it could be used. This consisted of stacking, watering (a spray can be seen to the right of the photograph) and turning regularly. The local policeman and a couple of friends kept themselves fit by doing the regular turning under contract.

A 'miners' feast', 1976. It was traditional in Shropshire that whenever a major project was completed, either on the surface or underground, a 'feast' would be held for the working miners. This might happen when a headgear was erected (called a 'rearing') or a tunnel completed. In this case a phase of redevelopment of the Tar Tunnel was complete and the tradition revived. Those attending were the staff and volunteers of the museum including the present Director of the Science Museum, London, and the author.

Shaft sinking at Shawfield Mine, Madeley, 1930. It was common practice in the coalfield to cover surface streams with brick arching and then form spoil heaps above. In the late 1920s such a culvert collapsed at the Shawfield Mine, damming the Wash Brook and causing extensive flooding upstream. The then landowners and operators of the adjoining Blists Hill Mine, George Legge & Son, were sued for damages by the local council and in 1934 went bankrupt. In the meantime an attempt was made at reopening the culvert by sinking a 70ft deep shaft through the spoil using a hand winch and forming a bypass tunnel around the collapsed section. (B. Waterson)

Shawfield Mine, 1917. The mine was probably sunk in the 1830s and until final closure, in around 1916, remained in the ownership of the Madeley Wood Company. In later years it was worked alternately, month by month, with Blists Hill Mine, less than 500yds away. During this later period the mine produced mainly fireclay from the productive measures at 158yds of depth although the shafts were over 220yds deep. The steam winding engine was of atmospheric type with a single, open-ended, vertical cylinder, 3ft in diameter by 4ft stroke. Steam was supplied at 4lb per square inch from the egg-ended boiler, which can be seen to the right of the house. Before this boiler was installed the haystack boiler on the extreme right had been used. The 14ft beam was of oak and drove the winding gear through a crank. (*The Engineer*, 3 August 1917)

A front view of the Shawfield Mine winding engine, with haystack boiler and chimney to the right. The ironwork was removed after the mine closed but the buildings remained, albeit rather collapsed, until the 1980s when they were vandalised and removed 'for safety'. Attempts had been made to save the engine house, as it was almost certainly the last surviving house that had contained a Heslop-designed engine. (*The Engineer*, 3 August 1917)

Hills Lane Mine spoil heap, c.1900. Hills Lane Mine was a sister mine to Blists Hill and Shawfield. All three lay alongside the local tub boat canal. Hills Lane Mine was probably sunk in the 1820s and the shafts were over 700ft deep. In 1842 a Child Employment Commissioner visited this mine and found a four-year-old boy at work underground. The mine employed about ninety men underground and twenty to thirty women on the surface picking ironstone nodules. This photograph gives an impression of the amount of waste produced (about ten tons for each ton of ironstone). The 'skeleton' bridge to the left carried the waste over the canal. The gasworks was opened using local coal in 1852. The pit finally closed about 1912.

A sunken tub boat and colliery crane stump, 1957. Much still remained of the colliery canal and tramway systems in the 1950s. This view shows the basin for turning and loading boats at Halesfield Mine with a sunken tub boat and a crane stump remaining. While this tub boat was made of wood, some were of iron and one of these can still be seen at the Blists Hill Museum.

Left: A flanged-rail plateway, 1954. The older Madeley Wood Company mines used trucks with 'penny wheels' and flanged rails. This example survived on a canal bridge at Blists Hill Mine until recently. Other lengths have been uncovered and preserved.
Right: A colliery wharf crane, 1959. Each mine had cranes such as the one shown, alongside the canal, road or railway This example was at Halesfield Mine and was used until the 1960s. The jib was of wood originally but this had been replaced by steel in later years.

Brick Kiln Leasow Pit mound, *c.*1926. This mine was a very old one, probably sunk in the 1790s and closed in the 1890s. It was 720ft deep and was often called the Lane Pit locally, after an older pit to which it connected. The photograph shows Matt Owen (with pipe), the company's head horse-keeper, and miner Sam Holcroft crossing the tip which runs alongside the Madeley to Ironbridge Road. In 1864 the pit was the scene of one of the worst local mine accidents; three men and six boys were killed when the winding chain became unhooked. They are buried in a communal grave in Madeley Churchyard.

The Brick Kiln Leasow Mine Disaster of 1872 involved the greatest number of casualties ever to occur at a Madeley Wood Company mine. Evidence was given at the inquest by owners William and John Anstice (brothers), James Davies, the mine manager, Joseph Vaughan, the engine driver, William Wallett, the banksman (son of one of the victims) and others. Two of the victims, Edward Wallett and John Tranter, had responsibility for management underground but they were both killed. The 'hooker-on' of the 'doubles', the loops of chain in which the miners sat, had apparently just clipped the hook onto the ring of the winding chain rather than through it. He was certainly one of those killed and could not be identified at the inquest since all the witnesses were dead. The pictures show the communal grave at St Michael's Church, Madeley, a copy of its memorial stone (below left) and a mourning card now in the Ironbridge Gorge Museum Collection.

IN
MEMORY OF

Edward Wallett   aged 52
Francis Cookson aged 13
William Jarratt   aged 18
John Farr   aged 14
Benjamin Davies aged 35
John Jones   aged 14
Joseph Maiden   aged 18
William Onions   aged 12
John Tranter   aged 37

Who were killed by the unhooking of the chains in which they were ascending the shaft of the Brick Kiln Leasow Crawstone Pit in this parish at the end of their day's labour on Tuesday, the 27th September, 1864.

"I went down to the bottoms of the mountains, the Earth with her bars was about me for ever: yet hast Thou brought up my life from corruption, O Lord my God".

"When my soul fainted within me, I remembered the Lord: and my prayer came in unto Thee, into thine holy temple". Jonah chapter 2 verses 6 & 7.

"Watch therefore, for ye know not what hour your Lord doth come". Matthew chapter 25 verse 13.

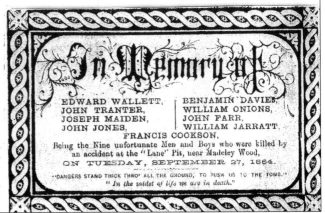

In Memory of

EDWARD WALLETT,   BENJAMIN DAVIES,
JOHN TRANTER,   WILLIAM ONIONS,
JOSEPH MAIDEN,   JOHN FARR,
JOHN JONES,   WILLIAM JARRATT,
              FRANCIS COOKSON,
Being the Nine unfortunate Men and Boys who were killed by
an accident at the "Lane" Pit, near Madeley Wood,
ON TUESDAY, SEPTEMBER 27, 1864.
"DANGERS STAND THICK THRO' ALL THE GROUND, TO PUSH US TO THE TOMB."
"In the midst of life we are in death."

45

Kemberton Mine, 1864. This was the last deep mine sunk by the Madeley Wood Company. It was 364yds deep and was completed in 1864, the date of the picture. The drawing is taken from a geological section of the shaft by William Ward of Madeley. It shows a typical outside winding drum and winding chain, supported due to its weight by 'rolley' posts. The head-frame behind the chimney is over a shallower shaft sunk for obtaining 'house' or boiler feed water.

Kemberton Mine, c.1900. A typical line-up of mine workers and horses in front of the shafts. In the middle distance can be seen the engine house, almost unchanged since 1864, while in the left-hand foreground is an unusual view of the squat ventilating furnace chimney. At this time the mine used over sixty horses and ponies underground. (F. Turner)

Kemberton Mine head-frame, 1945. This photograph shows the substantial tandem wooden head-frame constructed after 1912 following the expansion of the mine. Twin and tandem head-frames are a feature of the coalfield. Following expansion and concentration on coal mining, the mine employed about 600 persons, eventually increasing to over 800 after nationalization in 1947. Some ironstone was obtained, however, during the Second World War by hand-picking the waste rock as it left the mine.

Kemberton Mine's Samson coal cutter, 1946. This machine was used for undercutting the coal-seam so that it could be blasted down easily. Here, the machine was in use in a low development tunnel being used to form a new coalface. After blasting the coal was loaded by hand onto the conveyor at the left of the photograph.

Kemberton Mine winding engine house, 1947. The photograph shows the survival of probably the earliest engine house as offices. To the left of this is the later horizontal steam winding engine house, in use from 1912 to 1937, and behind it the house containing the electric winder used from 1937. This was the first coal mine in Shropshire to have an electric winder. Note the fencing of the field, made from old winding chain.

Kemberton Mine's tandem steel head-frame, photographed in 1967, shortly before closure. It is interesting to compare this view with the one from 1947 taken from roughly the same position.

Kemberton Mine shaft bottom, 1946. A line of tubs await their turn to be loaded onto the mine cage at pit bottom. The tunnel to the left connected the Kemberton Mine to Halesfield Mine.

Kemberton Mine shaft bottom, 1960. The shaft bottom had been reconstructed by this time and an automatic 'creeper' chain put in to avoid the necessity of manually pushing tubs uphill.

Kemberton Mine underground loading point, 1946. This shows a typical loading point, where conveyors from the coalfaces load into wooden waggons or tubs on the main haulage-way. An endless rope was used to draw the tubs or waggons to the pit bottom.

Kemberton Mine underground loading point, 1954. The coal from each district conveyor fell down a chute into a steel tub, which was marked for payment purposes with the number of the district. The steel tubs held 13cwt of coal. To the left of the photograph a diesel locomotive awaits for a train, called locally a 'journey'.

The opening of the new pithead baths at Kemberton Mine in 1941. These were the first pithead baths built by the Miners' Welfare Fund in Shropshire and 329th in the country. Those present were, from left to right, back row: -?-, W. Evison (farmer), E. Carney (engineer), N. Longworth (employee), W. Griffiths (employee), J. Yorke (employee), -?-, J. Cadman (son of managing director), A. Jackson (company secretary). Front row: G. Davies (District Miners' Agent), W. Lawther (National Miners' President), J. Cadman (managing director), -?-, J. Worthington (colliery manager), B. Ward (employee) and G. Whitehead (Kemberton Pit lodge secretary).

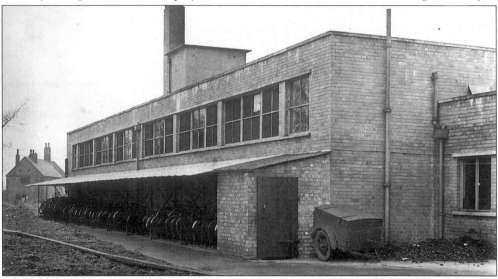

Kemberton Mine, rear of the new pit baths, 1941. This shows the special provision for bicycles which was trebled later. The baths had to be extended as employment increased from less than 600 to about 800 in the 1950s. The building still survives and was considered by Professor Pevsner in *The Buildings of England (Shropshire)* as being "architecturally specially interesting or important". The Welfare Fund's architect was J.H. Bourne, W. Evison, a local farmer, donated the land and the Madeley Wood Company agreed to donate half the "cost of coal, water, heating and lighting" towards running costs. The miners' committee had to find the remainder. In 1953 the Pithead Baths Committee was advised that they no longer needed to hold or raise funds as the baths would become the responsibility of the NCB, but the canteen, which was part of the building, remained the responsibility of the committee. The small cottage-style building to the left was the colliery offices.

Madeley Wood Company Rescue Team, July 28 1914. Rescue stations were set up at each principal colliery in Shropshire after 1906. The Lilleshall Company had the central station which held most of the equipment but this team, Team B, is outside the Madeley Wood Rescue Station Training Gallery. The gallery was the basement of the electric generator house, which once housed an 1870s steam winding engine. The building was built in the style of the Anstice Memorial Hall and survived until the 1980s. Only one of the rescue men is known – Sam Cookson, sitting on the left. There were three teams: A, B and C. The company was particularly keen on rescue as one of its rescuers had died some three years earlier while opening up part of the mine where there had been a fire. Mr Fred Ward was one of the first trained volunteer rescue men in this country to lose his life in rescue work. (Ironbridge Gorge Museum)

Madeley Wood Colliery First Aid Teams, 1955. This photograph was taken in the colliery training room. In the mid-1950s both senior and junior teams were frequent winners in NCB Area competitions. From left to right, back row: H. Lloyd (colliery first aid officer), team members D. Evans, P. Beddall, I. Brown, R. Rushton, A. Osborne (training officer). Front row: junior team captain T. Savage, Dr H.B. Upton (Area Medical Officer), senior team captain H. Mellor.

Officials of the Madeley Wood Company, 1941 – a pre-nationalization line-up. From left to right, back row: H. Brunt (overman), S. Thomas (overman), T. Franks (deputy), G. Haynes (overman), R. Cartwright (engineer). Front row: H. Hasledene (safety officer, later killed in the pit in 1950), H.S. Cockerill (under-manager), G.I. Scott (manager), Mr Staley (agent), J. Cadman (managing director), A. Jackson (company secretary), J.H. Brown (chief clerk), A. Stephan (electrician), E. Carney (engineer).

The Madeley Wood Colliery officials' staff party, c.1960. Several of the above-named will be recognizable here. It would appear that a good time was had by all. Such events took place annually and at other opportunities such as retirements.

A presentation at retirement, c.1947. A. Jackson, company secretary, presents deputy T. Franks with a clock to mark his retirement. Other officials present, from left to right, are H. Cockerill (under-manager), W.I. Cain (manager), and H. Brunt (overman). The ladies, from left to right, were Mrs Cockerill, Mrs Cain and Mrs Franks. Such events were almost always held in the clubroom of local public houses. These rooms were also the meeting places for Friendly and Benevolent Societies such as the 'Oddfellows' and the 'Buffs'.

Five miners at Madeley Wood Colliery, with a total of 217 years service, were presented with long-service certificates in around 1965. Area Group Manager H. Gittens presents A. Harris (centre) with his, marking 49 years. Others were, from left to right: A. Pemberton (40 years), A.V. Rickers (40), W. Griffiths (43) and T. Humphries (45). Behind the recipients were the Benevolent Committee members G.E. Whitehead (Lodge Secretary), J. Guy, H. Brunt (NACODS), A. Evans and E. Carney (engineers), G.T. Tullett (manager) and J.H. Brown (colliery clerk).

Madeley Miners' Welfare Recreational Hall, 1963. Unlike many large collieries the Madeley Miners did not have their own recreational hall until 1950, although they did have the use of the much earlier Anstice Memorial Hall (see p.29). The Miners' Welfare Fund was set up nationally in 1920 with contributions coming from the colliery owners and the coal royalty owners (at so much per ton produced). This was supplemented by a voluntary weekly levy on the miners. A recreation ground was established in most Shropshire mining towns in the 1920s and halls were built in St Georges (1929), Ifton (1932), Highley (1933), The Nabb (1936) and Hanwood (1938) but not at Madeley until the 1950s. Facilities inside the hall varied. At Madeley it was only a large meeting room with a kitchen, but the 'rec' had areas for football, cricket, tennis and bowls. Madeley Miners' Hall was demolished arond 1970 as part of the Madeley Bypass project. The fence was built to protect onlookers from flying cricket balls.

Madeley Miners' Welfare Children's Christmas Party, 1963. This was a well-attended annual event open to all miners' children and organized by a committee consisting of colliery management, officials and union leaders with other volunteers. Other activities organized by the 'Welfare' included sports days, a Youth Club, a Motor Club and some individual sports such as boxing. Normal works events, classes in first aid and occasional talks were held in the Welfare Hall as demand arose.

Madeley Miners' Welfare Football Team, 1950/51. During this season the team took on, and beat, a 'professional' team made up of Shrewsbury, Wellington and Birmingham league players on 3 May 1951. Pictured are, from left to right, back row: C. Chetwood (referee), H. Payne (chairman), W. Russell (trainer), D. Bradburn, J. Gwilliam, T. Hadley, R. Bridgwater, T. Sharack (committee member), N. Nickless, A. Payne (committee member), H. Lysons and J. Brown (secretary). Front row: J. Britland (committee member), A. Russell, R. Machin, T. Harris, B. May, R. James and D. Maddy. The club won many prizes during its twenty-five-year history (1945-1970), in particular in 1961/2 when it won the Hunt Charity Cup and the Clee Hill Cup. For much of the time there was a second or junior team also.

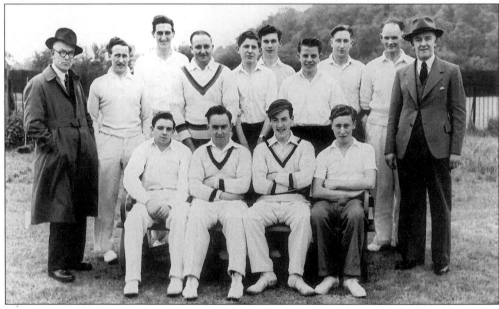

Madeley Miners' Welfare Cricket Team, 1951. This team played its first official match in 1951 and some of its players continued to play the team until their pitch on the Welfare Recreation Field was lost for New Town developments in 1968. The photograph shows, from left to right, back row: A. Jackson (club president), R. Wyatt, W.E. Rooker, A. Evans, R. Elcock, F. Jones, R. Lycett, E. Hadley, L. Bennett and W.I. Cain (colliery manager). Front row: P. Franks, A. Taylor, R. Jackson, P. Owen. (Mrs B. Rooker)

The colliery workers had their own Benevolent Fund to which each contributed a few pence each week. The photograph shows Jack Brown, honorary secretary, handing a 'benefit' to Ben Breeze, one of its oldest members, in 1963. He is assisted by Miss May Smart. It was stated at the time that since the then secretary had taken over in 1938 more than £8,600 had been paid out. The colliery canteen became an unofficial old miners' club each Friday afternoon and retired miners used every excuse and transport method possible to attend.

Madeley Wood Colliery's farewell party, 1967. Staff gather round and celebrate with tea (no alcohol was permitted at the colliery) as the manager , J.G. Tullett (right), shakes hands with the NUM Lodge Secretary, Norman Latham. The young lady present is the colliery manager's secretary and two surviving officers from pre-nationalization days are also in the front row, the colliery deputies' union leader, overman H. Brunt and the Colliery Staff Association representative, J. Brown.

Halesfield Mine, 1946. This mine was situated about half a mile from Kemberton Mine to which it was connected underground in 1939 as a wartime safety measure. Both mines were owned by the Madeley Wood Company. There were two pairs of shafts at Halesfield, sunk between 1840 and 1870 to a depth of about 300yds and previously called Old Hales (Tom Rowe's Pits) and New Hales. For many years the two pairs of shafts were worked independently, despite their depth, and old miners used to relate how they would send messages to their friends in the next pit by striking the solid rock with their picks. The mines were mainly ironstone producers and in 1895 employed a total of 160 men and women, the latter picking the ironstone nodules from the weathered shale on the surface. In 1912 ironstone production ceased following the closure of the company's Blist Hill furnaces but some coal was produced during the period 1920 to 1925. After 1939 the shafts were used solely for pumping from the combined mine, for use as upcast air shafts and as an emergency means of egress from the Kemberton Mine. The photograph shows the two head-frames at the mine. In the foreground to the left are the Lancashire boilers used for steam raising, to the right the 'new' fan house with the evasee chimney in front. The ropes for both shafts were operated from one winding drum – as one wound off the other wound on. Because of the great distance from the 'outside' pit to the winder an auxiliary pulley can be seen fitted to the inner pithead frame.

Halesfield Mine engine house and main shaft, 1946. The horizontal steam engine house and inner pithead frame. The pit is enclosed as it was used as an upcast, the air being drawn up by the fan.

Halesfield Mine, 1963. This view is similar to that from 1946 shown above. By this time the steam engine had been replaced by an electric winder and the old wooden head-frame by a steel one. In the foreground are the concrete covers over the two shafts of the Old Hales or Tom Rowe's Pits. When working under the 'chartermaster' system two of the shafts worked coal and two, ironstone. Tom Rowe, after whom two of the shafts were named, was one of the last chartermasters, or contractors, at the mine. The system of contracting whole mines out to chartermasters ceased in around 1900.

The demolition of Halesfield Mine in 1968. The head-frame was demolished in March 1968 and the remaining buildings, including the pit-top airlock (right), the fan (left) and the electric winder house, followed. The site is now a caravan park.

Exploratory drilling, Shifnal, 1955. Between 1952 and 1961 a number of deep bore-holes were put down to prove the extension of the coalfield to the east, near Shifnal. Most of these holes were put down by Messrs Craelius (later Atlas Copco), the Swedish drilling contractors, who used a 70ft drilling rig. The drilling rig shown was working on a hole near Haughton village. A professional paper was later published by the Institute of Mining Engineers giving the results from these drillings. (Institute of Mining Engineers Vol. 119 No.3, 1959).

On the drilling rig, 1955. The holes were made using the rotary method with cores being extracted from depths up to 1,500ft. The plant was entirely self-sufficient with its own diesel generator and diesel pumps for obtaining water from nearby streams. Drilling took place on a 24-hour basis, each eight-hour shift having a crew consisting of a master driller, an assistant, three labourers and a mud logger/core sampler.

Part of the Madeley Court Colliery, c.1906. This colliery, though almost surrounded by the Madeley Wood Company operations, was in separate ownership from its formation in the 1840s but by the 1880s various agreements for joint pumping took place leading to the transfer of mineral rights and some operations to the latter company in around 1900. Extraction of coal, ironstone and fireclay commenced near Madeley Court House around 1840 and in 1843 blast furnaces were constructed by James Foster. The furnaces continued to operate until 1902, supplied by mineral from shafts 1 to 17. All the shafts were worked under the chartermaster system. Ironstone production ceased in 1902 but some coal was produced until about 1910. In 1882 the surface equipment consisted of one pumping engine, seven winding engines and one 'old water engine'. All were steam-powered and of the beam type. (W. Harper)

Transportation of coal by tub boat from Kemberton Mine, c.1900. This section of canal, opened in 1792, was severed from the main coalfield tub boat system in the 1850s and from this time connected only the mines of the Madeley Wood Company to their brickworks and blast furnaces and, via the Hay Inclined Plane, to the Coalport China Works and the River Severn. The canal was extensively used for mineral transport until the turn of the century and finally closed in 1916. In the background can be seen the Madeley Court Company's blast furnaces and to the left the stack of one of that company's mines. W. Richards was the last tub boat operator. He is seen in the photograph holding the pole which prevents the boat hitting the canal bank. This boat sank in the late 1940s in very nearly this position (see page 43).

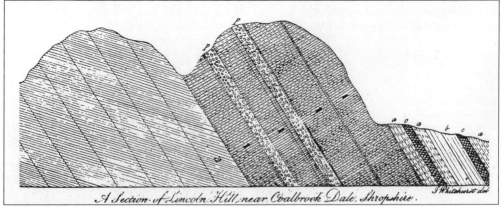

A Section of Lincoln Hill near Coalbrook Dale Shropshire.

Lincoln Hill Limestone Mine, Ironbridge. Silurian limestone has been worked since at least the early seventeenth century and by 1801 there were 'several prodigious caverns of limestone supported by stupendous pillars'. The mine was worked by adits from the side of the Severn Gorge and from several 30-45yd-deep shafts from the top of the hill. During the late nineteenth century the vast pillar-and-stall workings were opened to the public and are included on the list of attractions for travellers on the old Severn Valley Railway. The mining of limestone was continuous over at least a century and finally ceased in 1902. During later years only three men were employed producing about 600 tons per year. The beds were 30-40ft thick and dipped at an angle of 35°. This inclination appears to add height and vastness to the workings, which were, until recent backfilling works, still accessible to potholers. Donkeys were used for haulage underground, but little evidence has been found in the mines of the use of anything other than the simplest tools, shovels and wedges. The geological section of Lincoln Hill shown must be one of the earliest representations of this type made. It was drawn by John Whitehurst in 1786 for his *Inquiry into the original state and formation of the Earth* and clearly shows the inclination and variety of the beds.

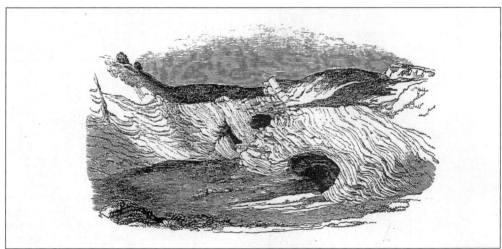

A sketch of quarries and mines at Lincoln Hill, 1839. In this illustration by R.I. Murchison in 'The Silurian System' the same features as shown above can be seen. According to this paper 'the dark shades indicate the places from whence the concretions or ballstones had been extracted' and 'on the right are the overlying coal grits'. The 'ballstones' were the purest, most valuable limestone for smelting. These were followed underground and the scene was still very similar before infilling commenced in the 1950s.

An adit entrance at Lincoln Hill, 1965. This is only one of several adits which have been constructed on hillside ledges above the now-ruined limekilns. This adit (probably dating from about 1800) can be followed for 35yd where it enters a limestone shaft at a depth of about 50ft. It is possible that this adit has been used also as access to a large kiln and this is still being investigated.

Lincoln Hill Mine, 1975. A member of the Shropshire Caving and Mining Club is standing on a heap of debris underground looking along the strike of the limestone bed towards a solid pillar of rock. These pillars are 20-30ft high and about 20ft square. Fourteen such pillars supported an area of working measuring about 110yds by 50yds. The mine has recently been backfilled. (D. Stevenson)

A limestone shaft head-frame near the top of Lincoln Hill, 1907. The shaft is 61yds deep and was last used early this century. It is believed that the shaft was sunk about 1800 and, according to J. Prestwich, a local geologist, passed through the lower seams of the coal measures. The photograph shows winding chain in evidence as late as 1907 although one of the head-frame's legs is definitely in need of repair.

A view in Lincoln Hill Mine 1975. A most unusual view of a mine, taken from the bottom of a 100ft deep shaft looking up to the surface, the circle of light at the top. The roof is unsupported and the shaft sides unlined. A mine explorer from the Shropshire Caving and Mining Club can be seen climbing down the wire rope ladder.

Four
The Lilleshall Company

The Lilleshall Company was formed in 1802 to continue the work of an earlier partnership (formed in 1764) between the Marquis of Stafford and the Gilbert brothers. Previously the partnership had been content to act as ground landlords to the mineral producers. Like the Madeley Wood Company, this concern became a multi-industry one, but on a larger scale, operating coal, ironstone, fireclay and limestone mines, blast furnaces, forges, brickworks and works for other clay products etc. The company lost its surviving mines, Granville and Grange, in the nationalization of the coal industry but was still operating a rolling mill, steel fabrication works and concrete brick plant in 1975. It continues in a much-reduced form but is no longer operating from a Shropshire base.

In 1871 the Lilleshall Company operated forty mines and produced 400,000 tons of coal, 105,000 tons of clay-band ironstone, 5,000 tons of fireclay and over 10,000 tons of limestone. The company also had fifteen pumping engines and raised nearly 2.5 million tons of water per month. Many of the mines used triple-linked winding chain with skips but a contemporary report states that they were introducing cages in order to increase production. The company made nearly all its own engines and patented an early mine ventilating fan. Both engines and fans were also supplied to other coalfields. By 1891 the Company was operating fifteen mines, in 1917 only five and at nationalization in 1947 just two, the Granville and the Grange, both near Donnington. These merged in 1952 and the combined colliery closed in 1979, the last surviving mine in Shropshire.

The history of Stafford mine is well documented. The first sod for the shafts was cut on 24 November 1842 after a ceremonial scattering of 'silver dewdrops'. Despite this, it was not until 8 December 1866, and many tribulations later, that the intended depth of 255yds was reached. The mine had four shafts and expanded to become one of the largest in the coalfield, employing over 400 men by 1905. After ironstone working ceased, however, numbers fell, until by 1924 only 270 remained. Coal production ceased in 1926 but pumping continued until 1939. This photograph is taken from a geological section scroll by T. Doody from around 1870 and shows the general surface arrangements when the mine was opened.

A close-up of one of the winding engines of Stafford Mine taken by George Watkins c.1930. It was a rotative beam engine, believed to be of Lilleshall Company make. It ceased work around 1938 and was scrapped. According to the mine engineer in the 1930s the engine had a 36in-bore cylinder with 6ft stroke, a 15ft winding drum and an 18ft-diameter flywheel. It operated on a pressure of 30psi. In later years the mine's second rotative beam winder was changed to a horizontal cylinder type with a crank on the rope drum shaft. The pumping engine was of the Bull type with a 45in-diameter vertical cylinder and 7ft 6in stroke. The piston rod was directly coupled to the pump rods but the engine was assisted by a large outside beam, which had a balancing weight in an iron tank. There were also smaller engines to supply the ten boilers with water and one to drive a rope that went down the shaft to work the underground haulage. All the engines at the mine were scrapped at the end of the Second World War.

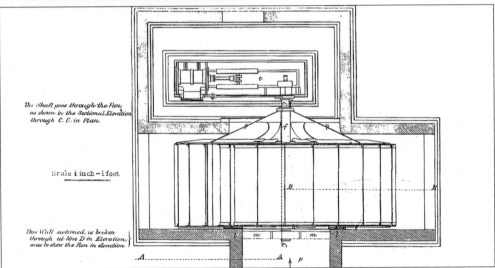

The shaft goes through the Fan, as shewn in the Sectional Elevation through C. C. in Plan.

Scale ½ inch – 1 foot

This Wall sectioned, is broken through at line D in Elevation, was to shew the Fan in elevation.

Lloyd's ventilating fan, c.1869. John Lloyd, after working at the famous Soho Works, Birmingham, joined Lilleshall Company around 1861. He managed the company's New Yard Works, which was soon producing railway locomotives, beam engines for pumping and winding engines. Many were for the company's own operations and Lloyd himself is said to have built for the Woodhouse Mine the county's first steam-powered ventilator, or fan, now known as the Lloyd Fan. The fan was 16ft in diameter and 5ft 10in wide and is said to have produced 59,400 cubic feet of air per minute. In 1869 the Company offered this type of fan for sale generally but only one other fan is known to have been made, for a Nottinghamshire pit. John Lloyd retired in 1904.

Woodhouse Mine, *c*.1920. This was in effect two mines, each with a pair of shafts, working coal and ironstone from shafts up to 311yds deep. In the 1920s this became a very large mining complex for the coalfield and in 1932 employed over 740 persons. For ventilation the mine first used a furnace, then a Lloyd fan. By 1891 this had been replaced by a 28ft-diameter Guibal fan running at 70rpm. No.1 Pit had a winding engine (right in photograph) with a vertical cylinder of 32in diameter and 5ft stroke, connected by crank to a rope drum shaft and two flat ropes. The drum was directly coupled to the crankshaft and the pistons went straight through the cylinders. It, too, is said to have been designed by Lloyd, the company engineer. Each cage held two 8cwt-capacity tubs. No.2 Pit winding engine had a pair of horizontal cylinders with cranks on the drum shaft (see p.70). No.1 Pit ceased production in 1931, No.2 in 1940, but some pumping was done until the 1960s using electric pumps. All steam engines were scrapped during the 1940s. This photograph is taken from a company catalogue of *c*.1920. It was unnamed but its identification is certain as this was the company's most modern and prosperous mine at the time. (Ironbridge Gorge Museum)

Woodhouse Mine remains, 1960. This photograph shows the large horizontal engine house and steel headgear as it was in 1960, by which time a small electric winder had been installed. The surviving buildings were removed in the 1970s.

Granville Mine, 1864, a drawing made by T. Doody and used to illustrate the geological section scroll. It shows one beam pumping engine and one vertical winder. The shafts had been sunk to 409yds by 1860 but one was deepened to 444yds in the 1950s to become the deepest in the coalfield. The mine was the last Shropshire mine to work under the chartermaster contractor system, by a Mr Cooper who retired in 1913. It normally employed about 300 men but reached a peak in 1967 at nearly 900 following the transfer of workers from Kemberton Mine when that mine closed. Granville itself closed in 1979.

Granville Mine, 1879. This painting by R. Williams was formerly in the surveyor's office at the mine. It shows that a second vertical winding engine had been added by this time. According to a former Lilleshall Company engineer, W. Atkinson, rotative beam winding engines were being used at both shafts in the 1930s. No.1 Pit had a single, vertical cylinder with a 32in diameter and 5ft stroke connected to the rope drum by a crank. Two flat ropes were used for winding, each rope raising coal from a different depth. No.2 Pit had a pair of engines with two vertical cylinders, each 16in in diameter, and two flat ropes. The mine also had a steam pumping engine of the Cornish type – with a 74in cylinder, 10ft stroke and steam pressure at 24psi. – and a 20ft-diameter, steam-powered Guibal fan which was in use before 1890 and replaced a furnace in the shaft bottom. (National Coal Board)

Granville Mine, 1944. The photograph shows that few changes had taken place since 1879. The coalfaces were now at some distance from the pit bottom and the company was considering sinking a new mine nearer their reserves. They were also planning a major reorganization but this was not completed until after nationalization. (Ironbridge Gorge Museum)

Granville Mine, 1949. This is a view taken from the other side two years after nationalization. Modernisation had begun with a new steel head-frame and electric winder house (to the left of the photograph) on the opposite side of the No.1 shaft to the original steam winder. The new electric winder, made by M.B. Wild, was the first electric winder to be ordered and installed by the National Coal Board. In the next few years all the old steam plant was replaced by electrically powered plant with new winders and pumps and new pit-top landing arrangements. Modern pithead baths, canteen, workshops and offices were also provided. (see photograph on p.126).

Above: A flat rope winding engine at Granville Mine, 1950. Granville Mine had two vertical steam engines operating flat rope winding equipment in the 1940s. Along with engines at nearby Grange Mine and Monkwearmouth Mine in the North-East these were said to be the last winding engines to use flat ropes in the nationalized coal industry. This photograph shows the vertical drive operating the crank lever with Mr T. Weston looking on. Flat ropes were 'spooled' on a reel layer upon layer, rather like cinema film.

Granville Mine's main haulage road, 1938, one of the few underground photographs found of this mine. It shows the old wooden tubs on a main-and-tail rope haulage system. The height of tunnels was later raised and larger one-ton-capacity steel tubs came into use.

Granville Mine's main transport road, c.1955. After 1953 a 2,500yd-long tunnel was driven beneath the existing workings to provide the main arterial roadway and intake airway for the mine. Along this roadway 12-ton electric-battery locomotives hauled new 2.5-ton-capacity mine-cars. At this time the workings were about two miles from the colliery shafts.

Opposite: Woodhouse Mine winding engine, 1945. This horizontal steam engine was chosen by the Lilleshall Company to be the replacement for the vertical winder at Granville after the closure of Woodhouse in 1940. The concrete beds were being prepared for it at the time of nationalization, but the new National Coal Board changed the plan and a 650hp electric winder by M.B. Wild was installed at Granville instead. The photograph of the disused Woodhouse winder shows its bi-cylindro-conical drum, a device which permits a torque advantage when winding commences and the load is at its greatest. (Ironbridge Gorge Museum)

Grange Mine surface arrangements, 1950. The Lilleshall Company began sinking the two 8ft-diameter shafts at this mine in 1864 and they eventually reached a depth of 320yds. The mine worked both coal and ironstone, and was probably the last mine in Shropshire to work ironstone in the 1940s. From the beginning, the pumping engine was similar to that at Stafford Mine. It was of the Bull-engine type, with a 42in-diameter cylinder of 9ft stroke working at 40lb pressure, and was non-condensing. The mine also had two steam winding engines and in later years a steam fan engine. In 1905 244 men were employed but by 1952, when the mine ceased production and was combined with Granville Mine, this had fallen to 162.

Grange Mine, 1964. At the time of the combination of these two mines in 1952-3, two 1000yd tunnels were driven to connect them. The recently installed modern fan at Granville was transferred to Grange and the former became the downcast, the latter the upcast for air circulation. Later, a methane drainage plant was also installed and a chimney constructed to discharge up to 600cu.ft of almost pure methane, although some was sold to the Gas Board. A training school was also built at this mine for new entrants. The mine head-frame still survives and the surface buildings have become the centre for a naturist park.

Grange Mine winding rope and shaft top, c.1950. This photograph shows clearly the wooden head-frame and two-deck cage together with the flat winding rope. The type of flat rope used was described in a technical paper by the NCB's chief engineer, B.L. Metcalf, in 1950. It consisted of six round ropes 'stitched' together as in his sketch (right). The photograph also shows a small winch drum that was used for shaft repair work.

Grange Mine winding engine arrangements. Over the years the winding arrangements at Grange Mine caused great interest. In 1870 the steam engine had a pair of horizontal cylinders, 15in diameter and 3ft stroke, and two 3ft-diameter drums for flat hemp rope. This was replaced by a 45in-diameter engine using a flat wire rope but the old one was kept and used to drive a haulage rope. Both engines were built by the Lilleshall Company. The photograph shows part of the cylinder, the drive and the flat rope reel. The use of flat wire rope continued at the mine until it ceased production in 1952.

Granville Mine fitting shop c.1952, prior to modernisation. Both Grange and Granville mine workshops changed little from Victorian times until as late as the 1950s. This scene in 1952 shows this clearly. The bench, workman's locked cupboard, small windows and overhead chain-operated crane were commonplace features at all major mines. Each workman had to buy his own hand tools. This also applied to workers underground who had to purchase shovels, picks (as well as paying for their re-sharpening), axes and even explosives until the 1960s.

Granville Mine officials' party, c.1970. One of the last 'presentation' parties for officials of the only surviving mine in the county. The photograph shows many officials who had transferred here from other Shropshire collieries upon their closure.

Probably Freehold Mine , Donnington, c.1880, from an unsigned painting formerly in the Surveyor's Office, Granville Colliery. The actual colliery is in doubt but there are some similarities with what is known of Freehold Mine. The mine was probably sunk in the 1840s. It had two 7.5ft-diameter shafts, the deepest reaching 734ft at the time of closure. When first sunk it was a small mine with 441ft-deep shafts and was ventilated by a furnace. It was mainly an ironstone mine which is further indicated here by the fact that the engines are at ground level and the shaft head-frames on top of the tips. This was caused when ironstone shale was spread around the pit mounds for weathering. For each ten tons of material wound only one ton of ironstone nodules was collected by the female pickers. The remaining waste was used as a surface upon which further ironstone shale was placed.

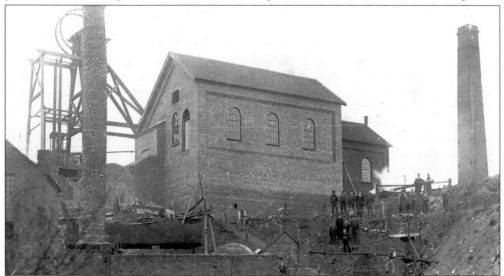

This view probably shows Freehold Mine in the 1920s. The mine closed in 1928 owing to heavy pumping costs. It had a steam pump and steam-powered winding engine. A larger one was installed for coal production in 1884. Little is known of any of the engines but the foundations were still visible until recently. The mine employed 203 workers in 1905, rising to 316 just before closure. The seams lay, in places, quite steeply – as much as 45° to the horizontal. Of particular note in the photograph is the tank in the foreground. It is likely that this was originally an iron tub boat as used on the local canal. One such boat, found being used as a water tank at a local farm, can now be seen at Ironbridge Gorge Museum. (R. Tranter)

Waxhill Barracks Mine, c.1900. One of the earlier Lilleshall Company mines, this was sunk in around 1818 and had a depth exceeding 300yds. The mine worked coal and ironstone and ceased production around 1900 although pumping continued until 1930. The pumping engine worked on the Cornish principle. It had a 61in-diameter vertical cylinder and was double-acting. The engine was scrapped in around 1940 but the remains of the engine house can still be seen. The photograph also shows two pit girls, making it the only known photograph showing females at work at a large Shropshire mine (see the detailed drawing on p.110).

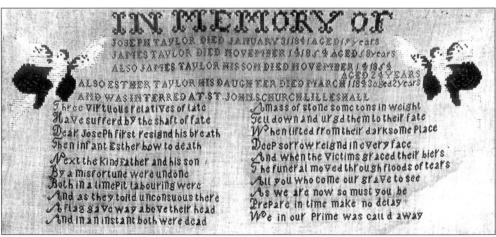

Lilleshall Limestone Disaster, 1854. A photograph of a sampler with a ballad commemorating the death of members of the Taylor family, two of whom died under a fall of limestone at the Lilleshall Company's limestone mine. James Taylor, aged 58, and his son, also James, aged 24, died on 14 November 1854 when 'a flag gave way above their head – and in an instant both were dead'. Four years later, on 16 October 1868, a similar incident occurred at one of the company's limestone mines killing three more men. (Ironbridge Gorge Museum)

Possibly Stephens Pumping Engine, Donnington, c.1900. This could be an earlier view from the other side of the engine in the photograph below. Note the 'wheel on a pole', the little headgear, the hipped-roof building and the square chimney. It would appear that the engine house was without windows on one side but had two on the other. In any case, the photograph is interesting because it shows the steam raising plant, the 'tenders' and the local tub boat canal. It also shows what appears to be an empty iron tub boat moored at the right of the photograph.

Possibly Stephens Pumping Engine, 1920. This mine engine by Donnington Wood church has been referred to as 'Poppitts' Pit Engine. It seems that in this photograph the engine was incidental to the persons in the foreground. The beam engine appears to be in good condition. Stephens Engine remained so until it was closed down in 1928, being scrapped shortly afterwards. It had a 52in-diameter cylinder and worked from a depth of 510ft. (Ironbridge Gorge Museum)

Possibly Woodhouse Mine *c.*1922. This is almost certainly a front view of the large engine house shown on p.67. It is especially interesting as it shows a Lilleshall Company horse in the charge of a known driver, Jack Fox. In front of the engine a group of about twenty miners pose for the camera and in the distance, to the right, can be seen the outline of St George's Parish Church.

A 'Notice to Horse Drivers' from the Lilleshall Company manager of Freehold, Granville and Grange mines, *c.*1920. The mines of the company used many 'horses' (which includes also ponies, mules and donkeys) both above and below ground. In 1927 Freehold Mine alone used thirty-six 'horses' alongside the 314 men employed. Accidents to the animals and their drivers were very common; indeed, at this time accidents to 'drivers' were the most common cause quoted and treated at the company's own hospital. In 1900 Shropshire mines employed 386 'horses' made up of 124 horses, 234 ponies, 26 donkeys and 2 mules.

LINES ON THE SAD ACCIDENT

AT THE

Donnington Wood Colliery Shropshire,

On Saturday Sept. 11 1875

1. Pray listen to these feeling verses,
   Which we now relate to you,
   At Donnington and miles around it
   There is much grief and misery too
   For eleven poor hard working colliers
   Went to labour under ground
   But by fire in the coal mine,
   A dreadful death they all have found

   It was at Donnington wood in Shropshire
   These poor colliers under ground,
   By a fire in the coal mine,
   A dreadful death they all have found.

2. To their work that fatal morning
   These poor souls their way did wend
   Little dreaming little thinking
   They'd meet with such a sudden end
   Down the shaft they all decended
   To labour for their daily bread
   And very soon it was discovered,
   That these poor colliers were all dead.

3. Some men both willing and brave hearted
   To save the sufferers then did try
   They risk'd their lives to search the workings
   And a fearful sight there met their eye

   Men who went down strong and healthy
   Now were found to be quite dead,
   All their troubles they were ended
   And their spirits they had fled.

4. Soon poor men and women assembled
   When the sad tidings they were known
   Freinds were looking for their comrades
   Relations looking for their own
   And when they brought up their dead bodies
   The sight was grievous to behold
   The anguish of their wives & neighbours
   No tongue can tell or pen unfold.

5. The dangers that surround poor colliers
   God in heaven only knows
   He ne'er is certain of returning
   When down beneath the ground he goes
   We hope their souls are now in heaven
   From their labour now at rest
   We hope they're happy with the angels
   And by their loving Savour blest.

A ballad published after the Donnington Wood Colliery Disaster of 1875, the second-worst such accident in the coalfield. It occurred at a chartermaster pit 'sited near the pool about 100yd past the cottages in Lodge Road'. The chartermaster was Henry Guy. The banksman responsible for shaft-winding at the pit where the fire occurred was also called Henry Guy. In fact, five of the eleven men who died underground were also called Guy and all are believed to have been related. It appeared that all eleven men and a horse had been overcome by fumes from an underground fire without anyone on the surface being aware of it.

Lilleshall Company Cottage Hospital, 1998. This building still survives in Albion Street, St George's, as a private house. It was opened by the company in 1903 after several years discussion, at a time when the Company was employing over 1,600 miners plus ironworkers and brick-makers, etc. Records at the Ironbridge Gorge Museum show that there were about thirty admissions each year. Of those, where occupations are listed, 75% of victims were either drivers (of pit ponies) or miners. The worst year for admissions was 1910, with fifty-three, but in its later years entries as low as twelve were made. The hospital closed in 1928. (Jane Wardropper)

The Shropshire Miners, Enginemen and Surfacemens' Federation motor ambulance parked outside Tranters' premises at St George's, c.1920. The federation included miners from most of the mines, not just those of Lilleshall Company. Paid-up members had to wear a lapel badge (note the two men on the left in dark coats). Tranters were, among other things, undertakers and the sign on the building seems to include the words 'neat turnout, prompt attention given'. A fourth generation still carries on this business. (Mrs M. Kent)

Coal distillation plant at Priorslee, *c.*1910. There has been a long history in the coalfield of the extraction of useful products from coal and shale. Most of the local ironmasters had plants for the production of coke and tar. Earl Dundonald's 'British Tar Company' was operating plants at the Calcutts and Benthall until the early years of the nineteenth century, at which time others were also experimenting with various systems of kilns and ovens. This photograph shows the first large, integrated system employed in the coalfield. A German company erected the plant and leased it to the Lilleshall Co. who later took it over. It used chamber-type ovens in place of the open heaps and circular ovens formerly used in the coalfield and lay between the Priorslee Furnaces and the Holyhead Road.

Priorslee Furnaces, 1864. Commencing in 1851, these furnaces became the company's principal furnaces and survived until 1959. Two of the steam blowing engines have been transferred to the Ironbridge Gorge Museum for preservation. The company had, at various times, other furnaces at Snedshill, Wrockwardine Wood, Donnington Wood and the Lodge, all using ironstone from the local mines. This illustration is from the head of the strata section scroll for the nearby mines.

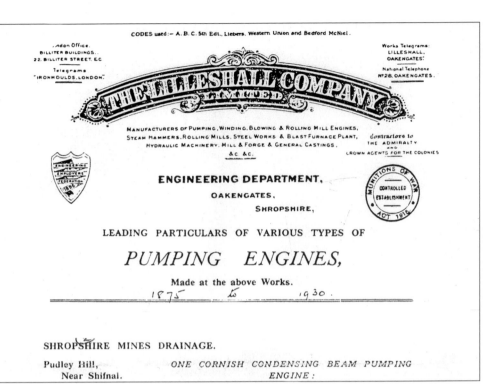

CODES used:— A. B. C. 5th Edt., Liebers, Western Union and Bedford McNiel.

London Office.
BILLITER BUILDINGS,.
22, BILLITER STREET, E.C

Telegrams
"IRONMOULDS, LONDON."

Works Telegrams:
LILLESHALL,
OAKENGATES.

National Telephone
Nº 28, OAKENGATES.

THE LILLESHALL COMPANY
LIMITED

MANUFACTURERS OF PUMPING, WINDING, BLOWING & ROLLING MILL ENGINES,
STEAM HAMMERS, ROLLING MILLS, STEEL WORKS & BLAST FURNACE PLANT,
HYDRAULIC MACHINERY, MILL & FORGE & GENERAL CASTINGS,
&c. &c.

Contractors to
THE ADMIRALTY
AND
CROWN AGENTS FOR THE COLONIES

ENGINEERING DEPARTMENT,

OAKENGATES,

SHROPSHIRE,

LEADING PARTICULARS OF VARIOUS TYPES OF

PUMPING ENGINES,

Made at the above Works.

1875   to   1930.

SHROPSHIRE MINES DRAINAGE.

Pudley Hill,
Near Shifnal.

ONE CORNISH CONDENSING BEAM PUMPING
ENGINE :

This heading from a 1930s sales catalogue introduces a list of pumping engines made by the Lilleshall Company between 1875 and 1930. The entry for one at the Pudley Hill Drainage Pit is shown, although there is good reason to believe this was in fact a reconditioned engine made earlier for the Wombridge Mines, Shropshire (see p.84).

The Pudley Hill engine house, c.1960. The photograph shows the remains of the engine house for the engine listed above. It was erected in 1890 for the Shropshire Mines Drainage Company, a 50-50 partnership between the Lilleshall Co. and the Haybridge Co., to drain the mines of both concerns. Built on an old colliery site about one mile from the works, the engine had a 66in-diameter cylinder and an 8ft stroke and pumped in three stages from a depth of 792ft. The engine worked for less than ten years. The house remains were removed in 1971.

82

A Lilleshall Company sales catalogue of 'Colliery Plant and Equipment', c.1960. The Lilleshall Company was still making mining equipment in the 1950s and 1960s. This included large new head-frames for a Nottinghamshire colliery and other more local ones. 'Kariscol' steel-framed winder houses and workshops, chutes, hoppers, winding cages and the mechanical parts of winding engines were also being produced.

COLLIERY
PLANT &
EQUIPMENT
by
LILLESHALL

A Lilleshall Company pit cage, c.1959. The company produced many single, two-deck and three-deck pit cages such as the one shown. One of their proudest claims at this time was that they had been the main contractors and fabricators for the reorganization of Granville Colliery, Leicestershire, a similarly named mine to one it had previously owned in Shropshire and which was still operating within a few miles of its works. The job of reorganizing the Leicestershire pit 'was completed during an annual holiday with no subsequent loss of time'.

Wombridge pumping engine house, 1964. Erected in 1858, this housed a 250hp Cornish beam engine built by Lilleshall Company for a consortium of local mine-owners who paid for it on a 'proportion by output' system. It could raise 3,388 gallons of water per minute with three strokes, though it was capable of up to eleven strokes per minute. The cylinder stroke was 10ft and the pump stroke, 9ft. Shortly after 1884 the engine was stopped because of a dispute between local mine operators over the 'proportion by output' system and the mines flooded. It is believed that the engine was then bought jointly by Haybridge Iron Co. and Lilleshall Co. and, after reconditioning, installed at the Pudley Hill Mine. The Wombridge mine was 175yds deep to the lowest coal-seam but old strata sections showed that it reached limestone at 197yds, which the miners may have worked also. Local tradition states that miners at one of the pits nearby, the Cats Head Mine, had to run from the incoming water whenever the pump stopped working.

The inclined plane at Trench, c.1910. This photograph shows the disused Wombridge pumping engine house on its prominent pit mound, a familiar sight to all who passed on road, rail and canal. The engine house was demolished by explosives for safety and development reasons in 1964. The inclined plane, by which canal tub boats were raised and lowered on trolleys, survived until the 1920s. The earthworks can, however, still be seen.

The Lilleshall Company's Donnington Wood Brickworks, 1968. The brickworks had the last chain-hauled tub system in the area. This was in use drawing tubs from a surface quarry to the kiln until 1971 but there had been many previous examples of this system on surface and underground. Each tub carried a raised 'notch' which the chain fell into, or rose from, automatically during the haulage operation. When not connected, such as at this right-angled bend and at the start and finish of the run, gravity was used to move the tub.

Lilleshall Company's Donnington Wood Kilns, 1968. This 'umbrella' kiln was a feature of the area until closure in 1971. The circular Hoffman kiln built in 1876 had a kiln diameter of 100ft and a chimney height of 100ft. It used about 1,800 tons of clay per month and required 4 1/2cwt of local coal for every thousand common bricks fired. There were thirteen chambers around the periphery, each containing 14,000 bricks. The fuel was added from the top of the kiln and the fire moved around the body of the kiln at about 17ft per day. At any given time, one chamber was being filled, one being emptied, three and a half smoking and preheating, three under fire, three and a half cooling and one empty.

Several long rows of single-storey, two-room barrack houses were built in the mining areas to provide accommodation for mine workers. They were built during the late eighteenth century and continued to be used until the 1950s. This photograph was taken around 1933. Barrack houses were located at Waxhill Barracks, Lilleshall Barracks and several other locations. The 1851 Census shows that at Waxhill Barracks, twenty of the twenty-seven single-storey houses had five or more inhabitants, while nine had seven or more.

Priorslee Village, 1950s. This small village was constructed around 1839 for mineworkers at the Lilleshall Company's Lawn and Rookery mines. It is now a 'conservation area' and the cottages have been modernised.

Five

More Mines North of the Severn

The major companies were the key players in East Shropshire but did not hold a monopoly. There were many small and even medium-sized companies operating alongside them, particularly in the nineteenth century. In 1891, for example, the Haybridge Iron Company operated ten mines, mostly about 500ft deep, and Hopley Bros' Wombridge Colliery had eight mines up to 200ft deep, but there had been other groupings before this, especially in the peak ironstone-mining days, including Botfield's Old Park, or Malinslee and Stirchley, Company and the Ketley Company. In the twentieth century, the mines have usually been worked in small groups of two or three and to relatively shallow depths, often less than 150ft. Due to this shallow depth, however, it has been possible to continue to use some of the simplest equipment – hand winches, horse gins and primitive steam engines.

By 1900 the era in which Shropshire was a leader in the country's mining industry was over and many of its skilled miners had emigrated elsewhere. The industry still employed nearly 4,000 people in 1905 but of these 1,600 were employed by Lilleshall Co. and 600 by the Madeley Wood Company. The remaining seventy mines in the Coalbrookdale Coalfield employed about 800 people, or about ten men each. Ten was the usual level for small mines for the rest of the industry's life.

There were still over twenty small mines north of the Severn registered as working in 1946, but this diminished in number rapidly thereafter until the last small mine closed in 1970. The photographs shown in the following pages are only a representative sample of the many little mines that worked within recent memory.

John Randall, RGS (1810-1910). Born in Broseley, Randall survived until the early years of the twentieth century and consequently saw many changes. Although he had no formal training in mining geology, he taught himself the subject and was, in later years, often called in as a consultant. In addition, he was an accomplished writer and produced several books including works on the clay industry and district histories, all containing much geological information. The book on his left in the photograph is said to be the volume on industry which he wrote for the *Victoria County History of Shropshire*. He was also a skilled bird painter in ceramics having worked for the celebrated Coalport China Company and in the Rockingham works. 'To his geological researches was due the extension of the mining industry in this neighbourhood' (epitaph, Madeley Church).

LAND,

AND

Coal and Ironstone Mines,

SALOP.

TO BE SOLD

BY

Private Contract,

ALL THOSE

TWO ADJOINING CLOSES OR PARCELS

OF

FREEHOLD LAND,

Called Astley's Furlong and Lower Meadow,

(PART OF ~~A~~ ~~~~ ~~~~ CALLED "THE BRANDS,")

TOGETHER WITH THE

MINES AND VEINS

OF

Coal and Ironstone,

IN AND UNDER THE SAME,

Situate and being at "The Brands," in the Parish of Stirchley, in the County of Salop, containing together by Admeasurement twelve Acres, or thereabouts, (be the same more or less,) and now in the Occupation of SAMUEL RODEN, as Tenant from Year to Year.

The Brands is only distant from Shiffnal three Miles, and from Ketley two Miles; the Land adjoining to the Stirchley and Ron Lee Colliery, and is within a Quarter of a Mile of the Shropshire Canal running to the Severn.

For a View of the Premises apply to Mr. RODEN; and for Price and other Particulars, to Mr. CORSER, Attorney, at his Office in Wolverhampton, Staffordshire.

An advertisement for land and minerals, 1852. Land could be sold with or without the minerals within it, or the various mineral beds could be sold separately. Advertisements such as this were common in the nineteenth and early twentieth centuries. This advertisement was for land used by the Stirchley and Randlay Mines.

BRANDLEE COLLIERY, HORSEHAY, SALOP.

A mining company letterhead, c.1935. One of the few illustrated letterheads that has been found, this one shows an unmarked railway wagon, though the company itself was never directly connected to a main-line railway.

Brandlee Mine, 1962. The Brandlee is a very old, shallow mining area with numerous shafts in a complex that extends over Horsehay Common to the Shortwoods. Mines on this site were at work throughout the nineteenth century but the mine shown was owned and operated by the Tarr family. One shaft, to the Clod and Randle seams at about 33yds, was sunk during the First World War. The other shaft was sunk to the Big Flint Seam at 8yds and later to the New Mine Seam at 13yds. Other shafts were sunk as the need arose. The corrugated-sheet-covered house contained a horizontal steam engine and vertical boiler, which was used until the mine closed in 1956. This was the last steam-operated winder at a working mine in Shropshire and it remained in position until it was scrapped in 1962.

A postcard showing a working mine and pit mounds, c.1900, one of the few such postcards produced in Shropshire to show a small mine. The mine must have been close to the site of that shown in the previous photograph. It seems to have had both a horse gin and a small steam winder as the hut shown is in line with the pulley. The large areas of flat mounds indicate that ironstone as well as coal had been worked, since small coal mines produced very little waste.

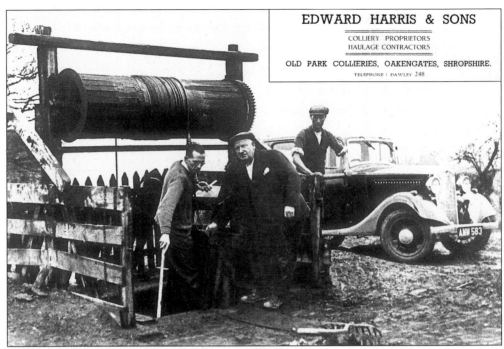

EDWARD HARRIS & SONS

COLLIERY PROPRIETORS
HAULAGE CONTRACTORS

OLD PARK COLLIERIES, OAKENGATES, SHROPSHIRE.

TELEPHONE : DAWLEY 248

Ivy Mine, Clares Lane, Ketley, 1934. This small mine was owned by Edward Harris (in the dark suit). The pit was 15yds deep and produced 36 tons of coal per week. The owners of this mine were among the first to use Bedford trucks for coal distribution. A letterhead for the company is also shown. (G. Harris)

Another 1934 view of Ivy Mine showing a second hand winch to the left of the picture. The photograph is believed to have been taken as a promotion feature for Bedford trucks. (G. Harris)

Harris's Old Park Mine, 1948, a general view taken just after the 1947 nationalization. A 'family' pit, this mine employed about twelve men including Albert Harris, the former owner, and his three sons, George, Len and Arthur (Arthur built the headgear). Also employed were three brothers named Lord. The mine closed around 1950. (G. Harris)

Another 1948 view of Old Park Mine. The steel head-frame was moved to Farm Mine, near Heath Hill, and more recently to the Blists Hill Museum where it can still be seen on the 'Miners' Walk'. The winding engine was electrically operated. Old mining tips can be seen to surround the mine; the photographer was also standing on one. A good supply of pit props lies in the foreground. (G. Harris)

Rock Fireclay Mine, 1964. Originally opened for coal in 1882, the mine was taken over by James Jones & Sons in 1928 to work coal, fireclay and iron pyrites but after 1956 only fireclay was produced. When the mine closed in December 1964 there was an electric winder and a hand winch at the two fireclay shafts respectively, a motorised hand winch at one of the coal shafts and two hand winches at the other. In later years the Clunch fireclay seam was worked from a 30yd-deep shaft using the pillar and stall system, the pillars being about 20ft square and the stalls, or headings, 6ft wide. The pillars were then robbed by driving further headings through them, 'splitting the pillars'. Hand boring machines were used for drilling shot holes and, after blasting, the clay was hand loaded and trammed to the pit bottom. Candles were in use for illumination and as a protection against running into accumulations of blackdamp. In the early 1960s the mine produced 150 tons per week and employed ten men.

Rock Fireclay Mine, 1965. This shows the main coal shaft's motorised hand winch and suspended box. The box was in fact the top of a mine tub. When carrying mineral, all three chains, two at one end and one at the other, were attached so that the box was level. When carrying people the box was suspended from two chains only so that it was at an angle as in the photograph. The rider then stood on the end of the box and held the winding rope. In the foreground is the 'tacking plate'. This wheeled platform was pushed over the shaft and loaded boxes were lowered onto it.

Underground at the Rock Fireclay Mine, 1964. Isaiah Jones, one of the two brothers who owned the mine is pictured just before the closure, resting against a rather suspect timber prop. His candle is in place in a gob of clay stuck to the prop and his jacket hangs opposite. Note the lack of height in this, one of the main tunnels. Isaiah was the under-manager/deputy for the mine as well as being a councillor and deputy chairman of Telford New Town Corporation.

Rock Mine 1964. The miner is hand-pushing a loaded wooden 'dan' – a shallow truck used because the roof was very low – to the pit bottom. These men were called 'dan-boys' or 'danners' and worked in a crouched position all day. Behind is another miner who had to get in tight against the side while the dan passed in these cramped conditions. The condition of the roof supports above the dan-boy can be clearly seen, as can the only illumination, the candles. Each candle (sold at sixteen to the pound weight) lasted about an hour in still air.

The fire bucket winch pulley and hand winch barrel at Rock Mine's No.2 coal mine, 1965. The smoke is from the fire bucket. This is the last known occasion that a fire bucket was lowered for ventilation purposes in a shaft in Shropshire. The mine used a separate hand winch for the fire bucket so that the hot bucket could be kept in readiness on the surface when men were down below. If blackdamp was found in quantity the miners could come up quickly on the other hand winch and the bucket could be lowered immediately. For safety reasons, the management never allowed both miners and fire bucket to be at the bottom of the shaft at the same time.

Rock Mine, 1965. After the mine closed, all the equipment, underground and surface, was salvaged by the Shropshire Caving and Mining Club. In order to get air circulating at the coal shafts a fire bucket had to be suspended down the shaft using the cast-iron hand winch. A Siskol coal cutter, purchased in 1937, was removed from the mine together with much other equipment dating from this time. This material is now at the Blists Hill Museum. Drawings and photographs of all the equipment have been preserved and a report published.

Shortwoods Mine, 1967. Situated on a site with a very long history of mining, this adit mine closed as late as February 1970, the last of several thousands of private mines to have operated in this coalfield. It was partly owned by Mr H. Tarr, who was also the manager. The adit shown is No.10 which was driven in 1953. Most of the other adits at this mine were still open and two were used for additional access and ventilation. The adit was driven from the outcrop of the Two Feet and Best coal-seams, which lie together at this point and have a combined thickness of 3ft. The pillar and stall method of working was used, the depth being only 23yds at maximum. A Siskol arc wall shearer undercut the Best seam in the 12ft-wide stall to a depth of 4ft 6in. The coal was then blasted and hand loaded into 10cwt-capacity wooden waggons, which were hauled to the surface by a small electric winch.

Shortwoods Mine, 1967. At the surface, the wooden tubs were hauled up a ramp by a direct-rope haulage engine (in the wooden hut behind the tub) and then tipped by hand towards the men in the photograph where the coal fell onto a screen.

Shortwoods Mine, 1964. The run of mine coal falling onto the screen bars was separated into 'lumps' and 'smalls', the latter passing through. In the hopper below, the lumps were sorted manually using 'franks' which were five- or eight-pronged forks. Large lumps were removed in this way for the prime coal markets.

Shortwoods Mine, 1964. Lorries reversed under the hoppers to collect their required product. The coal could be collected loose or bagged and went to the various industrial, domestic and power station customers as required.

The 'Rats Pit', Oakengates, *c.*1899. This beam engine stood beside the Great Western Railway between Wellington and Oakengates and was obviously derelict by this point. It has been identified as an early nineteenth-century, rotative, double-acting beam engine, geared for winding and possibly for pumping also. The photograph and description appear in *Trans. Shrops. Arch. Soc. Vol LIII*, 1949.

The Nabb Pit, *c.*1912. Whenever miners were not working at the larger mines, such as in disputes and layoffs, small 'jackey pits' were opened using any equipment to hand, in this case an old bicycle, a riddle, a bath tub and a spade. This mine was at the Nabb, St George's and was 7yds deep. Of the six men shown, four were the Edwards brothers (from the left: Harry, Charles, John and Alfred). The man holding the wheel was Albert Ryder, who married the Edwards' adopted sister May. The man on the shovel is unknown. The Nabb is an area of very shallow coal-seams, worked from early times, and was the site of the last planning application to work coal by underground mining in the 1970s.

ESTABLISHED 1780.   ESTABLISHED 1780

THE WOODLANDS & MADELEY WOOD
Broseley Brick and Tile Works
—— HEAD OFFICES ——
MADELEY, SALOP.
GEORGE LEGGE & SON,

MANUFACTURERS OF BROSELEY PRESSED ROOFING AND RIDGE TILES, IN VARIOUS COLORS, FINIALS, HIP, AND VALLEY TILES, PRESSED FLOORING SQUARES, DRESSED FLOORING BRICKS, BARN AND BREWHOUSE FLOOR BRICKS, BORDER TILES FOR GARDENS, AND ALL KINDS OF DRAIN AND SOCKET PIPES, FROM 2 TO 24 INCH, &c., &c.

A heading from a George Legge & Sons sales catalogue, 1930s. Red clays exist north of the Severn and have been worked extensively at the Woodlands, Ironbridge, in parts of Madeley and around Hadley, where there is still a large brick factory operated by Messrs Blockleys. George Legge and Sons was the last major company to mine and use the clays at the Woodlands (Ironbridge) and Madeley Wood (Blists Hill). They produced a wide range of brick and tile products including the famous 'Broseley Brick'. This was a type of brick made from particular clays on both sides of the river, not just in Broseley. The companies that made this type of 'Broseley Brick' protected their trademark very strictly.

View of Kilns and Works

KILNS FIRED WITH LOCAL COAL

PIPES MADE WITH SHROPSHIRE CLAY AND LABOUR

DOSELEY PIPE CO. LTD.

DOSELEY QUARRIES, DAWLEY, SALOP.   Tel. 362

London Office : 35 Crutched Friars, E.C.3.   Tel. Royal 4333

Doseley Pipes, c.1935. As well as quarries this company also operated mines and proudly proclaimed in their pre-war advertisements that they used local coal, clay and labour. The company's Randle Mine at Dawley employed up to thirty-five men at this time but underground working of coal and clay had ceased by 1955. Pipes of clay and other materials are still made at Doseley.

Six

Some Mines South of the Severn

This area could claim to be as old and, especially in earlier days, as important as that to the north. Here the seams of coal, ironstone and fireclay are at shallow depth and of good quality. They are, however, few in number, due to the unconformities and erosion that have occurred within the strata. The ironstone and coal were worked out early, the furnaces closed and industry then gravitated north-eastwards, except, that is, for the clay industry. Both fireclay and red clay have been worked widely right up to recent times.

The ironstone mines were exhausted early in the nineteenth century, the coal mines early in the twentieth century. All of these had been small operations. In 1891 there were eighteen working mines (eight coal, four fireclay and six red clay listed) while in 1905 there were nineteen (three coal, three fireclay and thirteen red clay) employing 119 men. No mine employed more than eleven men. By 1930 there were only seven mines listed, all clay mines, employing forty-nine men and in 1948 just three mines employed sixteen men. Opencast working continued, however.

The area south of the Severn is largely unaffected by the New Town developments so that more remains of the early mining industry can still be seen, although opencasting and the building of new housing estates has removed some evidence. Primitive mining equipment survived into the 1950s and 1960s, steam engines, hand winches and gin circles among them. Most of the evidence that can now be seen is from the later clay industry so that photographs naturally concentrate on this.

A view of the Jackfield clay industry, c.1898. The principal works shown is believed to be that of W & P Jones, known as the Hollygrove Brick & Tile Works. The company operated its own mines for red clay in the vicinity of the old church at Broseley Wood. A horse gin at one of these mines can be seen at top right. The shafts were at the Hollygrove and the Rock and were about 33yds deep. Clay was often brought to the surface further down the hillside by means of an adit. (R. Miles)

Guests Deep Mine, Broseley, 1951. This was a very old mine and probably the mine described as 'a Deep Pit on Crompton's Land' in a deed of 1726. The shafts were about 150yds deep and while, in later years, the mine was mainly for red clay, it had also produced some white clay and a little coal. In later years too a 'fat grey glacial clay' was also produced from a quarry near the shaft top. For tile making this was added to the red clay in the proportion of 2:1 red to grey. The mine rarely employed more than eight men producing about twenty-four tons of clay per week. The clay was got by hand and loaded into 10cwt trucks which were then trammed to pit bottom. It took five minutes for the engine to raise each tub. The mine closed in 1941, until which time it continued to be furnace ventilated. (F.R. Gameson)

Guests Deep Mine, 1951. The mine cage was suspended from the pulley on a wooden head-frame. The shaft was fenced for safety after the mine closed. (F.R. Gameson)

Guests Deep Mine, 1951. The winding engine was of great antiquity; the design and some parts were believed to be 130 years old. It consisted of a single, vertical cylinder with a 15in bore and 38in stroke and was double-acting. The piston was connected to a 10ft 6in-long, cast-iron beam, pivoted at its centre. The crank transmitted power to the two cable drums, of different diameters to wind from different depths in the shaft, which geared in as required. The engine worked on a pressure of 5lb per square inch, steam being produced originally in a haystack boiler but later in an egg-ended boiler. Attempts were made to preserve the engine but since it represented no particular period of development these failed and it was scrapped. (F.R. Gameson)

A typical advertisement for clay products, early twentieth century.

Deep Pit, Broseley, c.1930. This mine supplied Broseley's Milburgh Tileries with clay. The shaft was over 100yds deep and when the clay reached surface it was still 'rock hard'. The weathering clay heaps are shown to the left of the workmen. The trucks in use all had 'penny wheels' and ran on flanged rails.

A horse gin at Deep Pit, Broseley, c.1940. This photograph is the most recent available of a horse gin in the coalfield. The gin is interesting because it was constructed very simply, of un-barked timbers, and it had only one rope which wound on and off the drum as required. It is known that at least one horse gin was in use in the coalfield near Madeley as recently as 1948. (P. Kendrick)

A 1936 close-up of one of the mine waggons used at the Broseley clay mines. This had penny wheels and was used on flanged rails. The sides are shallow to allow it to be used in underground roadways of very little height. The two hooks are for lifting purposes, when tipping, but there was usually a third hook, in the centre at the opposite end, so that the whole waggon could be raised in a level position in a shaft without a cage. Note how the two sides have unworn timber inside while the end is much worn by tipping and by using it for riding. When used for riding only two chains are hooked to the waggon .The third is left hanging free so that the waggon is suspended at 45 degrees for men to stand in. (P. Kendrick)

Reward notice, 1914. C.R. Jones and Sons were concerned at the amount of vandalism even in 1914 but there had also been at least one case locally where a rope had been partially cut through during a weekend and men had been killed.

ONE GUINEA Reward.

WHEREAS some evilly-disposed Person or Persons, during Sunday, October 11th, Removed the Covering of a Coal Pit Shaft at Benthall, Salop, and threw the Covering together with a Chain and Wire Rope, down the Shaft, causing serious damage to Messrs. C. R. JONES & SONS, and endangering the public.

The above Reward will be given by the Broseley Association for the Prosecution of Felons to any Person giving such information as shall lead to the conviction of the Offender or Offenders.

F. H. POTTS,

Broseley, 14th October, 1914. Treasurer.

Printed by SLATER & CO., The Works, Iron-Bridge.

Miners' strikes brought much hardship to the miners, their families and the remainder of the working people. This photograph shows family groups setting out from Cape Street, Broseley, in around 1912 to seek outcrop coal in the surrounding countryside. (D. Oakley)

Wartime coal mining, c.1916. This is one of a group of at least four similar photographs showing local people digging coal at Fox Holes, Benthall. (Footridge is a local name for a drift or adit mine.) The photographs show people of all ages with sledges, riddles, full and empty sacks, shovels and picks. It is said that the lord of the manor, who was both land and mineral owner, allowed this work to alleviate suffering. On some photographs Lord Forester is present as is his son, Captain Forester, with his young wife, and on one the local policeman, PC Edwards, stands in uniform, looking on.

A hand winch at Rowton Farm, near Coalport, 1984. This was said to be over one of the ventilation shafts of Gitchfield Mine, which was worked from an adit by the railway line at Coalport. Clay was produced here for William Exley's Coalport Tileries. The mine was unusual in that both red clay and fireclay were worked, the fireclay being in a seam 25ft below the red clay. In 1920 the clays were mixed on the surface for use in the proportion of 4:1 red clay to fireclay. The mine closed around 1950 but the hand winch on the ventilation and escape shaft remains virtually intact. (I.A. Recordings)

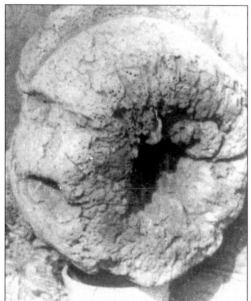

This flanged, wooden waggon wheel was found in a Broseley mine in around 1930 and is something of a mystery. Wooden railways had been used in Shropshire since the early years of the 1600s. These earlier rails were of the flanged type and the wheels that ran on them were flat discs of wood. During the 1720s the Coalbrookdale Company began to cast iron plate wheels and in 1767 began to use cast-iron rails also. Later, flanged wheels were introduced. Similar metal flanged rails and plate wheels were in use in Shropshire mines until the 1950s (see p. 44). The transition from wood to metal and of the flange from rail to wheel was obviously a slow process but it is most odd that early wooden wheels such as the one in the photograph should exhibit the flanged shape commonly regarded as a later development. The blackpowder can on the right, made by a local creaftsman, was also found in a mine.

Tuckies Hill engine house, 1979. This early nineteenth-century steam engine house was probably for a mine, but all that is known is that it belonged to the mine-owning Maws family in the 1880s, by which time it had already been converted into a house. During renovation in 1983 it was closely examined and found to have the conventional engine house form: three storeys and a cellar. On the ground floor, holes went through the walls into what was the boiler house. The first floor is supported on two massive beams which have 3ft 6in-diameter arcs cut into them to take the cylinder. The north-west wall is about 4ft thick, strong enough to form a pivot for the beam. There are also two timber beams, high up and cut off at the wall face, which probably supported a gallery. The photograph shows the front of the engine house with the hole for the beam bricked up but still with its wooden lintel.

A limestone miner's cottage, Church Aston, 1965. This seventeenth-century, thatched, 'one-up-one-down' cottage was formerly maintained by the Shropshire Caving and Mining Club, a group of mining and caving enthusiasts, who used it as a base from which to record and explore the mines of Shropshire and the surrounding counties. General repair work located several mining relics in the actual structure including the use of flanged rail as door lintels. The artefacts shown around the building have all been salvaged from local mines; in the foreground lie the remains of a horse gin. All these relics have now been moved to the Ironbridge Gorge Museum.

Seven

A Mining Miscellany

There are many aspects of mining that can be studied by mining enthusiasts and social historians and a few are noted in the following pages. Miners' housing has always been a popular topic and a wide range of type and standard has been found. The miners' union has always formed an interesting case study and mementoes and monuments are easily found in an area like Shropshire. The study of women in mining is popular, but researchers often overlook the part played by ironstone pickers on the pit mounds as in Shropshire. Miners' Welfare has been dealt with in passing in this book but could provide a subject for study on its own. Education in mining and mining schools has been passed over even in this book not for lack of information but because of lack of space. The principal mining school operating in Shropshire was based on the old Walker Technical College, Oakengates, opened in 1927 (though mining classes started long before this). As well as fitting out drawing offices and lecture rooms, the Miners' Welfare Fund provided an equipment package consisting of a gas fired boiler, an experimental Marshall's steam engine, a gas engine, an electric motor and generator and an experimental fan. For many years the remarkable Reynolds-Anstice collection of minerals and fossils was held at the Oakengates College but was later transferred to Shrewsbury Museum.

There are many other areas of interest that could be tapped relating to the mines, for example, land reclamation and ecological aspects of derelict land, but the most popular options still seem to be 'family history' and 'accidents'. Anyone interested in the wider aspects could do no better than study the many publications of the Shropshire Caving and Mining Club, a group established in 1959 and now with over 100 members, which has amongst its aims the study of all aspects of Shropshire mining underground and on surface. The address can be obtained from branches of the County's libraries.

Squatter-type housing at Madeley Wood. The mine operation needed workers; the workers needed homes. The owner could allow the miners to squat, provide houses or leave it to speculators. In the Coalbrookdale Coalfield in earlier times the owners 'permitted' squatting , the miner building his own house using any material available to him. In the example shown, single-storey cottages were constructed on a disused ironstone spoil heap some time around 1800. Other miners converted disused workshops or engine houses or built simple thatched dwellings as on the opposite page. In later years rows of 'barrack houses' and terraced houses were provided, examples of which have been given previously in this book.

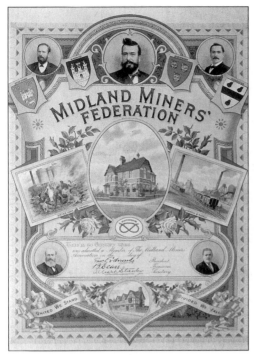

The Miners' Union

There appears to have been a County 'Association' of miners in the 1860s and by 1873 there was a Shropshire branch of the Amalgated Association of Miners but the national association collapsed soon after. Shropshire was present at a further national conference in 1880 and shortly after became a member of the Midland Counties Federation of Miners. The Shropshire Miners' Association was officially formed in 1886. From then until about 1930 William Latham was its secretary and official representative at national conferences. By 1899 the Midland Counties Federation had become the Midland Miners' Federation. Shropshire, though small in membership, played a major part in this. At one time three of the six leading figures had a Shropshire background. The membership certificate shows two Shropshire men in around 1893. Top right, next to the Shropshire emblem, is Albert Stanley, the Cannock Chase miners' representative (born at Dark Lane and a Shropshire miner for many years) who became the federation's secretary. Bottom right is Albert Gough, the Shropshire miners' representative. At this time the south Shropshire miners would join the South Staffordshire Branch and north Shropshire miners, the North Wales Branch. Below is the Salop Miners' Federation lapel badge of 1914 . This indicated to all the wearer's membership. The 'L' has been said to be either the proof of payment in the 'L' quarter of the year or membership of the 'Lilleshall' branch or lodge. (Ironbridge Gorge Museum)

Granville Lodge votes to return, March 1974. Miners of the Coalbrookdale Coalfield usually supported the national union's calls to strike. The photograph shows a vote in favour of returning to work after the strike of 1974.

Laying up the Shropshire branch NUM banner, 1979. On Friday 29 June 1979, as Shropshire's last mine was closing, the Granville Colliery Lodge handed over their banner to the Ironbridge Gorge Museum for safekeeping. The point was stressed that this was a loan not a gift as one day a new mine might open. At a small ceremony alongside the re-erected Harris' pithead frame the colliery manager, in full mining dress, flanked by the Lodge Secretary and Lodge President, carrying a pick and shovel respectively, formally handed over the banner to the Museum Director. Thus ended a short parade through the town of Madeley when the last 200 members, in ranks of four, wearing white pit helmets, followed their banner. All had memories of happier days, since just twelve years before their branch had had over 2,000 members.

Agreement, between the MADELEY WOOD Co., LTD., and the LANCASHIRE, CHESHIRE AND NORTH WALES (INCLUDING SHROPSHIRE) COLLIERY DEPUTIES' AND SHOTFIRERS' ASSOCIATION. *15/-*

1. The wages of Firemen shall be 13/- per day (plus the present flat rate allowance of 1/- per day—plus the national advance of 8d. per day), and the wages of Shotfirers 11/*£* per day (plus the present flat rate allowance of 1/- per day—plus the national advance of 8d. per day), and shall not be subject to percentage variation under the system of Ascertainments, but shall be subject to negotiation between the parties hereto.

2. No overtime rates whatever shall be paid.

3. Firemen and Shotfirers shall be afforded an opportunity of working six days per week. When not required to carry out their statutory duties, they shall perform such work, (other than getting coal for purposes of sale), as may be required of them by the Management.

4. Firemen and Shotfirers shall be entitled to six consecutive days holiday with pay each year. A Fireman shall be required to work on Bank Holidays only for carrying out necessary statutory duties, or in case of emergency. Recognised Bank Holidays shall be:—Christmas Day, Boxing Day, Good Friday, Easter Monday, Whit Monday, August Bank Holiday.

If required to work on any one of these days, the Fireman shall be given a holiday on some alternate day.

5. Coal allowance to continue as at present, and to follow local custom.

6. Four weeks notice on either side shall be given before terminating contracts of employment, except for misconduct.

7. In the event of a Fireman or Shotfirer meeting with an accident, he shall be allowed the difference between the amount of compensation and half wages for not more than four weeks in any one year, thereafter compensation in accordance with the Workmen's Compensation Act.

8. When a Fireman or Shotfirer is off work through sickness, he shall be paid £1 per week for not more than four weeks in any one year, on production of a Medical Certificate.

This clause to operate for a period of six months from the date of this Agreement, and if found to work satisfactorily, to be extended for a further period of six months.

9. Any difference that may arise in connection with the carrying out of this Agreement shall be referred for settlement to the joint committee representing both sides.

SIGNED, For and on behalf of the Madeley Wood Co., Ltd.

J. G. CADMAN, Managing Director;
J. WORTHINGTON, Manager.

HENRY D. BRUNT,
Madeley Branch Secretary;
JOHN DAVIES, District Secretary;
W. T. MILLER, General Secretary.

November, 1939.

Pages from a deputy's membership book, 1939. The deputies and shotfirers had a separate union, later to become part of the National Association of Colliery Overmen, Deputies and Shotfirers Associations. These pages show the conditions agreed in the immediate pre-war period. The colliery administration staff had a special branch of the NUM to cover their interests – the Colliery Officials and Staff Association. In post-nationalization days it was obligatory for all mineworkers to be union members.

Women in Mining

Even after the legislation of 1842 banning the use of women underground, women have played an important part in Shropshire mining and, at the ironstone mines, sometimes made up one third of the labour force. Among all the mines there were 551 females working in 1880 from a total workforce of 4,781 and during the twenty years before this date, of about 300 mineworkers killed, five were female. Over the years the greatest number of female deaths have been caused when women assisting at the pit-top accidentally fell down the shaft. One of the mines inspectors noted that banning women from underground had increased the number put in hazardous working areas on the surface. The photograph shows a detail from an 1847 drawing by W.W. Smyth (see p.31) giving the earliest known illustration of women working at a Shropshire mine.

There are only two known pictures of pit girls in their work attire. This one is a modern sketch by Malcolm Newton taken from a photograph believed to be of Waxhill Barracks Mine in 1900. There are several descriptions of their dress but these are not always consistent as it appears that they wore whatever they could find. E. Onions of Oakengates told the Select Committee on Mines in 1865 that the girls 'were dressed in frocks and petticoats', they had leggings to keep their feet and stockings dry and 'did not wear trousers like men'. The Employment of Children Commissioners in 1842 said that they wore 'handkerchiefs around their necks with hats or bonnets on their heads'.

Shropshire pit girls in the fields of Harlington, 1906. Several reports describe how the pit girls 'come up to London in the month of May, and go for three months into the service of market gardeners'. Some suggest this migration was because there was no frost on the pit mounds to break down the shale into nodules of ironstone and clay. However, E. Jones, Lilleshall Company's manager, told a Select Committee in 1866 that he had to 'release' girls in the summer to make jobs available for some underground miners, who would otherwise become unemployed when demand for coal was lower. To get to London in the 1840s, the girls would have had to walk over 100 miles. This picture is taken from a set of photographs now in the Ironbridge Gorge Museum Collection which shows the 'Shroppies,' as they were called, travelling among the strawberry fields in Harlington, Middlesex. (S.J. Hayward)

Anny Payne, Shropshire's last ironstone pit girl, 1987. Mrs Anny Payne was born in 1887 at Malinslee, then lived in Dawley. In 1900 she went to work at the Madeley Wood Company's Kemberton Mine. Her mother had bought some print and made a bonnet and a bag apron. She also bought a pair of nailed boots and a new basket to carry her lunch in. At work the blacksmith made her an iron box with two handles which she had to carry on her head using a roll of old stockings. Her job was to collect the nodules of ironstone, put them in her box and carry it to the heaps. 'It hurt.' She retired to get married before 1910 but she retold her story many times before she died aged 103 in 1991. (Ironbridge Gorge Museum)

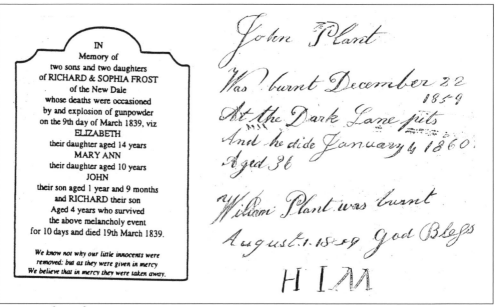

IN
Memory of
two sons and two daughters
of RICHARD & SOPHIA FROST
of the New Dale
whose deaths were occasioned
by and explosion of gunpowder
on the 9th day of March 1839, viz
ELIZABETH
their daughter aged 14 years
MARY ANN
their daughter aged 10 years
JOHN
their son aged 1 year and 9 months
and RICHARD their son
Aged 4 years who survived
the above melancholy event
for 10 days and died 19th March 1839.

*We know not why our little innocents were
removed: but as they were given in mercy
We believe that in mercy they were taken away.*

John Plant
Was burnt December 22 1859
At the Dark Lane pits
And he dide January 4 1860.
Aged 36

Wiliam Plant was burnt
August 1 1859 god Bless
HIM

Memorials and Mementos

Left: The Frost Memorial, Wellington. Accidents bring great sadness to a mining community but also a great feeling of togetherness. Ballads have been written, (the writer has collected about ten and published some in an Ironbridge Gorge Museum publication) but solid memorials last longer. Two communal graves were referred to earlier but there are other memorials, perhaps even more poignant. The Frost Memorial in All Saints Churchyard, Wellington, is dedicated to the children of Richard Frost, who was presumably in charge of a mine. He kept gunpowder in his own home for safety but unfortunately it ignited and the blast caused the death of four of his children aged fourteen, ten, four and one.

Right: An inscription from a family Bible at Old Park giving details of the demise of two loved ones.

It is surprising what old miners keep to remind them of earlier days. For example, the badges and tokens given to a Kemberton Mine employee in the last decade of that operation – a safety reminder badge, rescueman and first aider badges, an identification badge and the obligatory twin metal tallies with his number to permit access to the mine.

Eight

The Forest of Wyre and Clee Hill Coalfields

The Forest of Wyre Coalfield, though of relatively little economic or historic importance, is the largest in Shropshire, being about 50 square miles in area. It extends down the Severn Valley from Bridgnorth to the Abberley Hills. Coal-seams have been worked in both the Middle, or Productive, Coal Measures and the Upper Coal Measures. The coal-seams in the Upper Coal Measures are sulphur-rich and generally of poor quality.

The lower Middle Coal Measure group of seams crop out to the west between Billingsley and Kinlet but die out south of Highley. The principal seams are named after their general thickness: Five-foot (or Brooch) Coal, Half-yard Coal, Four-foot Coal and Two-foot Coal. The Upper Coal Measure group of seams have been worked on a small scale on the Shropshire/Worcestershire border but especially around Bayton and Mamble.

Although mining had taken place at least by the seventeenth century, it was all small scale. At the beginning of the nineteenth century some larger mines were commenced at Billingsley and Highley although working was intermittent. The *Report of the Commissioners into the Coal Trade*, 1871, showed that collieries were in operation at thirteen places in the coalfield, although not all were in Shropshire. The total output of the district was given as 15,000 tons of coal per year, very small compared with over a million tons per year in the Coalbrookdale field. The reasons for the low output were given as the railways enabling 'sweeter' coals to be brought into the area and mineral owners charging too high a royalty. The situation improved considerably after the discovery of the deeper, low-sulphur seams in the local coalfield.

In the 1870s there were three significant collieries, at Billingsley, Tasley and Harcourt, and a later Government report of 1891 shows Highley Mine at about 900ft deep and Billingsley at 500ft. In 1905 Highley Mine employed 307 people, Kinlet 259 and Billingsley 29, while in 1921 Highley employed 477, Kinlet 362 and Billingsley 266 (though it closed that year). In the 1930s, a new mine at Chorley was opened but this was short lived. In 1940 the Alveley Mine commenced. There were also at various times up to six mines employing less than ten men each, mainly in the 1920s.

Highley Mine railway sidings, 1938. The coming of the Severn Valley Railway in 1862 was highly beneficial for local mines. Highley, Billingsley and Kinlet were all connected to the line and had their own wagons. (T.H. Stonehouse)

The Highley Mining Company was formed around 1873. Its first shafts were at Highley Mine, which commenced production in the late 1870s. This project was successful and in 1890 the Company opened a second mine at Kinlet, about two miles south-west of Highley. In 1915 the Company took over the ailing Billingsley Mine two miles away but this was not a success. Billingsley closed in 1921 and Kinlet in 1937, but Highley Mine continued until 1940 when it was replaced by the company's newest mine, at Alveley on the opposite side of the River Severn.

Kinlet Mine in the 1920s. Sinking at this mine commenced in around 1890 to the Brooch Seam, a seam of good-quality coal about 3ft 9in thick. A large steam winding house with engine was built in 1896. During the First World War 300 employees produced about 320 tons of coal per day. The mine closed in 1937. (R.E. Evans)

Billingsley Mine, c.1915. The mine was in an old mining area and in 1891 was operated by the Severn Valley Colliery Company with two shafts up to 500ft deep and 7.5ft in diameter. By 1905 the mine employed about twenty-five men. In 1910 it was purchased by the Billingsley Colliery Company who redeveloped it but this company ran into financial difficulties due to the steepness of the seams and geological faulting. In 1915 the Highley Mining Company took it over, having already taken over the Garden Village housing development intended for the Billingsley workers. By 1914 the mine was employing 243 persons and just before its closure, in 1921, 277 were employed. (Shropshire Records and Research)

Highley Mine's twin head-frames in 1938. The mine worked the Brooch Seam from shafts about 900ft deep. During its life the mine generally employed 400 to 500 men and to accommodate them long terraces of houses were built in Highley village (the longest consists of thirty-five two-storey houses). The village was probably the county's most archetypal mining community. (T.H. Stonehouse)

The upcast airlock, Highley Mine, 1938. The box-like arrangement around the shaft prevented short-circuiting of air, the air being drawn up this shaft by the fan. The head-frame is of the modern steel type and the mine trucks, at about one ton of capacity, were quite large for their time. The Brooch Seam was relatively soft and could be cut by hand picks, but in 1917 Hopkinson chain coal cutters were introduced. During the First World War production reached about 450 tons per day.

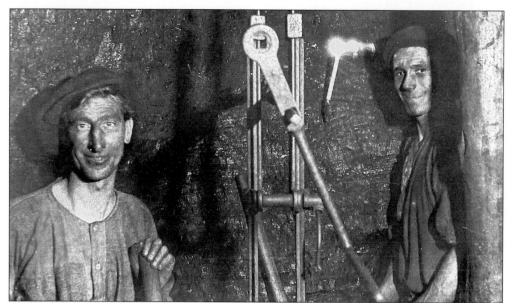

Drilling shotholes for blasting at Highley Mine, 1919. The machine is a hand-operated screw drill and the operators are J. Jones (left) and W. Hall. Notice the candle in the 'gob' of clay; candles were in use underground until the 1920s. The screw machine shown replaced the old method of 'punching' shotholes with a hand punch. (F.W. Beddoe)

A Highley Mining Company locomotive, c.1900. The company had its own steam locomotive, bought in 1896 from Andrew Barclay of Kilmarnock and named *Kinlet*. It has been renamed and is now at the Ironbridge Gorge Museum where consideration is being given to reverting to the original name. The locomotive was very new when the photograph was taken. (Mrs Viggars)

Shaft sinking at Alveley Mine, 1937. By the end of the nineteenth century the workings at Highley had proved the reserves on the opposite side of the River Severn. In 1937 the Highley Mining Company sank a large shaft, about 377yds deep, to develop these reserves and this was to become the company's main production shaft. The combined mine was nationalized in 1947 and subsequently equipped with the latest machinery. Later, however, the mine suffered geological difficulties, especially with regard to roof control, which prevented further mechanisation and the mine was closed as being uneconomical in January 1969. During the mid-1950s Alveley mine employed over 1,250 men but this had fallen to 700 shortly before coal production ceased. At its peak the mine produced about 300,000 tons per year, as against 500,000 tons from the whole Coalbrookdale Coalfield at that time. (T.H. Stonehouse)

Alveley Mine, 1938. A close-up of the shaft collar being formed. Only the top of the shaft was square, the rest was circular. The head-frame was made of concrete and Alveley was the only mine in eastern Shropshire to have this type of head-frame. Winding was done electrically. (T.H. Stonehouse)

Alveley Mine pit bottom, 1967. Around 1960 the shaft bottom was reconstructed to accommodate larger underground trucks, called mine cars, of 2.5 tons capacity. Modern equipment was also installed to mechanise the loading and unloading of the cage. This photograph shows the general arrangements with two small supply cars awaiting dispatch.

Alveley Mine's main haulage road, 1967. This was also constructed during the 1960 reorganization so that men, mineral and material could be transferred more quickly and efficiently between the coalfaces and the pit bottom. Electric battery locomotives were purchased with a centrally located cab. One of these is shown in the photograph.

The mechanised coalface at Alveley Mine, 1967. In the last few years the coal was cut and loaded at the coalface by a shearer machine and the broken coal transported by the chain conveyor shown. The roof was supported by hydraulic props and long metal bars, not, as in former years, by wooden props and wooden bars or short metal 'straps'.

The journey from pit bottom to coalface was made easier by the use of carriages, as shown. These were drawn by a locomotive and the operation was under the control of a 'guard' as on standard railways.

A photograph of Alveley Mine just prior to closing, 1967. Part of the colliery operations on the other side of the river can be seen on the extreme left. The supplies compound lies to the front of the picture. Many of the buildings remain and the site is now occupied by small industrial units and a country park.

Alveley Mine's aerial ropeway, 1967. The two parts of the mine, Alveley, with its production shaft, and old Highley Mine, on the opposite side of the river, with its coal preparation plant and railway siding, were joined by both a bridge and, after 1960, an aerial ropeway. The ropeway carried the mineral in buckets and, on the Highley side, had a right-angled bend so that the buckets then travelled a short distance parallel to the river to the coal preparation plant. The buckets were of the drop-bottom type.

One of the last shifts at Alveley Mine, 1968. The closure of the mine with the loss of 571 jobs finally came in January 1969 after a number of on/off announcements. The reason for closure was given as 'geological difficulties' leading to a loss of £92,000 in seven months, a period which, in itself, had been one of reprieve from an earlier proposed closing date. There were serious fears of increased unemployment in the village as 148 of the 571 miners to be made redundant were over fifty-five years old.

Highley Miners' Welfare Hall, 1933. As befits an archetypal mining village, Highley was provided with a fairly conventional but well equipped Miners' Welfare Hall and recreational area. The hall itself seems to have changed little outwardly since it was opened on 24 June 1933, having been built at a cost of £1,892 (including furnishings). It was built to accommodate 260 people and was provided with 'cloakrooms, kitchen, store and verandah'. The designer was R. Whitfield Parker.

Hunt House Mine, 1970. Just a mile outside the county boundary, the Hunt House Mine was a modern, private mine. The first shaft was sunk by four brothers, G.R., E.T., P.H. and H.W. Mole in around 1954. In 1960 the mine, operated aptly by Mole Mining Ltd, employed thirty men underground and fifteen on the surface, and produced 30 to 50 tons of coal per day. An electric winder was used to raise coal from the Five-foot Seam through the 61yd shaft. This photograph seems to show a split seam with a thick dirt band in the middle. This is being cut out by a miner using a compressed-air pick. (Worcestershire County Council – County Museum)

Hunthouse Mine, 1970. This photograph shows all the main items of plant in proximity to the winding shaft with its modern steel head-frame. When the company closed the mine in 1972 an attempt was made to work it as a miners' cooperative but the mine closed completely in early 1973. In October 1973 it was sold for £38,000 but following the fuel crisis of that time was soon being offered for sale again at £100,000. (Worcestershire County Council – County Museum).

Bayton Mine, c.1910, a photograph from an original postcard. This mine, like Hunt House Mine, is just outside the county boundary but has been included for completeness. Many mines, with shafts and adits, have been worked under this name in this remote border country and its miners are noted for their tough individuality. The largest mine in later years was Bayton No.6, which employed more than seventy men in 1948 but was closed in 1950 by the National Coal Board as 'uneconomic'. Bayton No.6 had been opened around 1938 to replace Bayton No.3 which was worked on a nearby site from 1924.

The Cleehill Coalfield

This really consists of two small, isolated coalfields centred on the Brown Clee and the Titterstone Clee respectively. The coal-seams, lying immediately beneath the basalt (or 'dhustone') cap of each of the hills, have been worked from early times and the remains are the nearest Shropshire has to the conventional 'bellpit' workings. Some parts of these coalfields are over 1,700ft above Ordnance Datum and for this reason they have been described as 'the highest in the Kingdom'.

The Brown Clee Coalfield is about two square miles in area and contains three principal coal-seams, the Jewstone Black, the Threequarter and the Batty. All underground extraction appears to have ceased by 1900.

The Titterstone Coalfield is about four square miles in area and is, in turn, made up of a number of smaller areas of working centred on the localities of Knowbury, Catherton, Cornbrook and Clee Hill Village. Five seams have been worked and these are, in general, thicker than those of Brown Clee. Some ironstone has also been worked and Carboniferous Limestone has been mined and quarried south of Clee Hill Village. The last coal mine in the coalfield closed in 1927. Limestone was last worked underground in the vicinity in 1914.

A characteristic feature of the miners of the South Shropshire coalfields was their part-time nature. Many, even in recent years, worked in the mines and, at the same time, ran small holdings 'on the hill'. It was not uncommon for the smaller mines to have to close down at certain periods of the year for such work as lambing and harvest to be undertaken.

Catherton Common area, 1963. The photograph shows the remains of bellpit-type workings at Lubberland on Catherton Common, Titterstone Clee Hill, in 1963. The encroachment of smallholdings onto the common is also clearly shown. (Cambridge University Press)

Watsall Mine, *c*.1900. The photograph seems to show a single steam engine drawing from several positions. The shaft to the left has a head-frame carrying a pulley which is obviously connected by rope through the single rolley post to the engine. There is an empty winding drum at right angles to the direction of pull – unusual but possible. There appears to be an angled guide pulley in line to support this change of direction but how it works is not clear. The following note from a mine inspector's report of 1853 shows that such conditions did exist: 'when an engine is drawing from 5 or 6 pits at the same time and some of them 300 yd away how can the engineman keep his eye on three pits at once?' (K. Beddoes)

The management and men of Watsall Mine, *c*.1900. The photograph shows those involved with the operation of the mine, including twenty-nine men, five horses and two dogs. The two men on the left are sitting on upturned riddles. In 1891 this mine, near the 'three-forked pole' on Titterstone Clee, had two shafts, 330ft and 246ft deep, and worked the Smith Coal-seam. The manager was T. Edwards. In 1905 it employed thirty-five men but it had closed before 1917.

Index of Mine Locations

Note - where no grid reference is given there are a number of possible positions.

A photograph of Granville Mine taken shortly before closure in May 1979. Granville was the last underground mine to operate in Shropshire.

Selected Bibliography

Anon. 'The Reconstruction of Lilleshall & Madeley Wood Collieries', *Colliery Guardian Vol. 187*, 6 Aug 1953.

Alfrey J. & Clark C. *The Landscape of Industry (in the Ironbridge Gorge)*, Routledge, 1993.

Brown I.J. 'The Coalbrookdale Coalfield', *Catalogue of Mines and Mining Bibliography*, Shropshire County Library, 1968.

Brown I.J. 'The Mines of the Madeley Court Company', *Shropshire Archaeology Society newsletter No.38*, 1970.

Brown I.J. 'Mineral Working and Land Reclamation in the Coalbrookdale Coalfield', Ph.D. Thesis, Leicester University, 1975.

Brown I.J. *The Mines of Shropshire*, Moorland Publishing, 1976.

Brown I.J. *Shropshire Tragedies - a Collection of Ballads*, Ironbridge Gorge Museum, 1980.

Brown I.J. 'Early Attempts at Land Reclamation in the Coalbrookdale Coalfield', *Environmental Managers' Journal Vol. 3 No.4*, 1995.

Brown I.J. 'Underground in the Ironbridge Gorge', *Industrial Archaeological Society Journal*, 1998.

Brown I.J. 'The Lloyds', *Industrial Archaeological Review Vol.14*, 1991.

Brown I.J. 'Geology and Mining in Telford – A Review', *Proceedings of British Society of Soil Science*, September 1998.

Clark C. *Ironbridge Gorge, English Heritage*, Batsford, 1993.

Coxhill D.J. *The Limestone Mines of Lilleshall and Church Aston, Shropshire*, Shropshire Caving and Mining Club, 1992.

Davies S. 'Rural Colliers of Wyre', *Folk Life, Vol. 22*, 1983-4.

Evans R. & Poyner D. 'The Wyre Forest Coalfield', *Cleobury Chronicles No.3*, 1994.

Frost A. *Death and Disaster in Victorian Telford*, AJF Publications, 1995.

Gale W.K.V. & Nicholls C.R. *The Lilleshall Company 1764-1964*, Moorland Publishing, 1979.

Hamblin R.J.O., Brown I.J. & Ellwood J., 'Mineral Resources of the Coalbrookdale Coalfield', *Mercian Geologist Vol. 12*, 1989.

Hamblin R.J.O. & Coppack B.C., 'Geology of Telford and the Coalbrookdale Coalfield', *British Geological Survey Memoir*, 1995.

Jenkins A.E. *Titterstone Clee Hills*, privately published, 1982.

Mugridge A.J. *Twelve Mines in the Broseley Area*, Orchard Press, 1992.

Pearce A. (ed) *Mining in Shropshire*, Shropshire Books, 1995.

Prestwich J. 'On the Geology of Coalbrookdale', *Transactions of the Geological Society of London. Series 2 Vol.5 Pt.3*, 1840.

Price G.L.A. 'Coal Mining in the Clee Hills', *Transitions of the Birmingham Enterprise Club Vol.2*, 1968.

Raistrick A. *Dynasty of Ironfounders (The Coalbrookdale Company)*, Longmans, Green & Co., 1953.

Trinder B.S. *The Industrial Revolution in Shropshire*, Phillimore, 1973.

Trinder B.S. & Brown I.J. *The Coalport Tar Tunnel*, Ironbridge Gorge Museum, 1972 (reprinted).

Trinder B.S. *The Industrial Archaeology of Shropshire*, Phillimore 1996.

Williams D.H. 'Vertical Sections through the Coalbrookdale Coalfield', *British Geological Survey Vertical Sections No.23*, first published 1846.

The compiler has written substantial articles on aspects of mining in East Shropshire in several journals including the following:

In *The Shropshire Magazine*: a series of twelve articles on various aspects between January 1962 and May 1966, 'Rock Fireclay Mine' October 1966, 'Madeley Wood Colliery' February 1967,

'The Miners' Revolution' January 1968, 'Blists Hill Mine' May 1974, 'Women mineworkers' June 1990.

In the *Special Accounts, Yearbooks, Annual Journal* and *Quarterly Newsletter* of the Shropshire Caving and Mining Club: 'Limestone Mining' 1966, 'Mining Ballads' 1966, 'Rock Fireclay Mine' 1973, 'Springwell Mine Disaster' 1974, 'Shawfield Colliery' 1979, 'Lincoln Hill Limestone Mine' 1981, 'Early Mining Maps' 1995, 'Reopening Old Shafts on Titterstone Clee c.1880' 1995, 'Novel Mining Methods in the Forest of Wyre' 1995, 'William and John Anstice, mineowners' 1996, 'Power House at Kemberton Pit' 1996, 'John Lloyd & Lilleshall Company' 1996, 'Miners' Welfare Fund' 1996, 'Shropshire Pit Mice' 1996, 'Shropshire Mining Schools' 1997, 'William Latham, Miners' Agent and the Union' 1997, 'Three Highley Miners' 1998, 'Blists Hill Colliery and the Tar Tunnel' 1998, 'Meadow Pit Colliery' 1998.

In the *Bulletin* and *Mining History* publications of the Peak District Mines Historical Society: 'Mineral Wealth of Coalbrookdale' 1965, 'The Chartermaster System' 1992, 'The Mining Community of Cuckoo Oak and the Madeley Wood Mine' 1991 and 1992, 'Limestone Mining at Ironbridge' 1995, 'Kemberton Pithead Baths' 1996, 'Underground Canals in Shropshire Mines' 1997, 'Ironstone Working in the Coalbrookdale Coalfield' 1998.

In *British Mining*, a publication of the Northern Mines Research Society: 'Mineral Working and Land Reclamation' 1979, 'Horses in Shropshire Mines' 1989, 'Women Workers at Shropshire Mines' 1989.

Details of the availability of the above publications can usually be obtained at local libraries or from the National Association of Mining History Organizations c/o Peak District Mining Museum, Matlock Bath DE4 3PS. Tel.(01629) 583834.

The Shropshire Caving & Mining Club. Anyone wishing to know more about the Shropshire mines could do no better than contact this group. The group was formed in 1959 to study and explore the disused mines in Shropshire and has more than one hundred members. Its activities include mine exploration, surveying, history, publication, photography and video recording, geology and preservation. The club also supports all aspects of the national codes on mine access, safety provisions and protection of historic remains. Addresses for contact with the club can be obtained from Shropshire libraries or from NAMHO (address as above).